## Also by Lanza del Vasto

Return to the Source   (1972)

Principles and Precepts
of the Return to the Obvious   (1974)

From Gandhi to Vinoba:
The New Pilgrimage   (1974)

Warriors of Peace   (1974)

# MAKE STRAIGHT
# THE WAY OF THE LORD

# MAKE STRAIGHT
# THE WAY
# OF THE LORD

*An Anthology of the
Philosophical Writings of*

## LANZA DEL VASTO

*Translated from the French by
Jean Sidgwick*

Alfred A. Knopf   New York   1974

This book contains selections from the following works by Lanza del Vasto:

*Return to the Source*: Copyright 1943 by Editions Denoël, Paris. English translation copyright © 1971 by Rider & Company, London. Reprinted by permission of Schocken Books, Inc., New York.

*Principles and Precepts of the Return to the Obvious*: Copyright 1945 by Editions Denoël, Paris. English translation copyright © 1974 by Schocken Books, Inc., New York. Reprinted by permission of Schocken Books, Inc.

*Chansonnier Populaire*: Copyright 1947 by Editions du Seuil, Paris.

*Commentaire de l'Evangile*: Copyright 1951 by Editions Denoël, Paris.

*Le Chiffre des Choses*: Copyright 1953 by Editions Denoël, Paris.

*Les Quatre Fléaux*: Copyright © 1959 by Editions Denoël, Paris.

*Approches de la Vie Intérieure*: Copyright © 1962 by Editions Denoël, Paris.

*La Montée des Ames*: Copyright © 1968 by Editions Denoël, Paris.

*L'Homme Libre et les Anes Sauvages*: Copyright © 1969 by Editions Denoël, Paris.

*Eclats de Vie*: Copyright © 1973 by Editions Denoël, Paris.

Library of Congress Cataloging in Publication Data

Lanza del Vasto, Joseph Jean (Date)
Make straight the way of the Lord.

1. Meditations. I. Title.
BV4832.2.L32    242    74–7739
ISBN 0–394–49387–7

Manufactured in the United States of America

First Edition

# CONTENTS

## Contents *vii*

## PART THREE: SOCIAL REALITY, UTOPIA, THE KINGDOM OF HEAVEN

# Contents

# PUBLISHER'S NOTE

Today Lanza del Vasto is the acknowledged leader of the nonviolent movement in France. But the seed was sown in 1936, when he left Europe for India in search of true spiritual values. It was there that he met Gandhi, who bestowed on him the name Shantidas (Servant of Peace). Although Lanza would have preferred to remain at Gandhi's feet, he realized that he must return to France and do there what Gandhi had done in India—train a small band of followers to make a stand for justice and for truth. He tells of this pilgrimage in his book *Return to the Source.*

Toward the end of the Second World War Lanza formed a select group that worked together in Paris, and in 1948 the first rural community, the Community of the Ark, was set up at an estate at Tournier. The Ark is a nonsectarian order, open to people of all religions providing they adhere strictly to the tenets of their faith; it is a working order of men and women who put Gandhi's principles into practice in their daily life. The note that is sounded constantly is this: "The aim of manual labor is not only to obtain one's daily bread by pure means, but to bring about an inner harmony of body and soul." An effort is made to apply nonviolence at all levels, for, as Shantidas stresses, one cannot demonstrate nonviolence in public if one has not yet achieved it in the privacy of one's own home. It is always a question of inner preparation and strength. The Companions of the Ark take vows of nonviolence and dedication to truth, vows of purification, poverty, service, work, responsibility, co-responsibility, and obedience. These vows are renewed each year.

In 1953 the community moved to Bollène, and ten years later they set up their home at la Borie Noble, 2000 acres of mountainous farmland in the Cévennes. At the present time, there are two communities of families living there, working on the land, spinning, weaving, and carving. There are now also offshoots of the Ark in Morocco, Belgium, Canada, and Argentina. Living in each community, apart from the Companions who have taken vows, there are novices, and young people who are interested in the aim of the order and have come to train for short periods. In addition, throughout France there are Friends of the Ark, who are sympathetic toward the order and organize seminars on and campaigns for nonviolence. In February 1958, a separate organization, Nonviolent Civic Action, was set up to unite people of differing views within the movement who are dedicated to nonviolent political action.

In 1958, ten years after the Ark's inception, thirty Companions and novices went to Paris; together they fasted, chained to the railings around the obelisk in the Place de la Concorde, to show their determination to end the atrocities being committed in Algeria by both the French army and the Algerian rebels. From that time on, the Companions have demonstrated continually against torture, against internment camps, for the right to conscientious objection, and, of course, against the Bomb.

This book is a selection from ten of Shantidas's twenty-three works published in France. It contains the essence of his teaching, his philosophy, his way of life.

# PART ONE

---

# IN SEARCH
# OF THE SELF

## WARNING

A book cannot teach you how to dance.

Nor how to meditate.

Honesty requires me to put you on your guard, as far as possible, against illusion, disappointment, and misunderstanding.

For reading is not enough to learn how to live, which is the subject of this book. You will still need somebody by your side to guide and watch over you, encourage you or teach you moderation at the right moment, someone respectful of the originality in every man. And you will need the warmth of friendship.

These things cannot be put into words. They can only be transmitted by living example or by bringing the searcher to discover their truth by himself, within himself.

In any case, the real subject of all these talks is silence.

They were given to the Companions of the Ark, men and women who live in a community bound by vows and a rule of life, and also to groups of Friends of the Ark, who live in town like other city-dwellers, and to the guests who joined us at the great feasts or in our summer camps: visitors concerned with what to do with their lives.

The talks were taken down in note form and for years

circulated only among private groups in a newssheet entitled *News of the Ark*.

Not without misgiving have they been delivered up to the hazards of publication. Nevertheless, it is hoped that even an unprepared reader will find something true, strong, and good in this book. May it awaken in him a desire to know more about our way of life and, above all, a desire to put it into practice, the better to serve truth, justice, and peace.

This collection of notes is far from being a systematic, methodical, and complete treatise. Two of our chief exercises, fasting and vigil, are only mentioned in passing. The following books also deal with the doctrine of the Ark: *Principles and Precepts of the Return to the Obvious;\** A *Commentary on the Gospel,†* like this book a collection of talks; and *The Four Scourges,‡* a study of the nature and destiny of civilizations and the civic duties of spiritual man.

The teaching of the Ark is not properly religious. It neither opposes nor replaces any religious teaching. Its task is a much humbler one, although indispensable, universal, and often neglected. We do not put ourselves above, or against, or beside, but below.

Our business is "to make ready a people prepared for the Lord." The truths we reveal cannot spring from the asphalt of current morality and current philosophy. We are asphalt breakers.

There is nothing personal in our teaching. Its value is

---

\* Published in New York by Schocken, 1974.
† Published in France by Editions Denoël.
‡ Published in France by Editions Denoël.

without proportion to the merits or demerits of its spokesman. He is not giving something of his own to his fellow men, but rather calling them to give themselves to and live by the doctrine to which he has given himself, and which has given him life. All he has done is plant and water. "So then neither is he that planteth any thing, neither he that watereth; but God that giveth the increase" (1 Cor. 3:7).

You will see that the book is studded with quotations from the New Testament and allusions to the Bible. There could be even more. If the scriptural references which confirm every point of our teaching had been given—and particularly the most paradoxical of these—they would have filled a volume of equal size.

You will also find quotations from sages who do not belong in our tradition, but it would be a mistake to conclude that what you are reading is a syncretic anthology of maxims, precepts, and advice taken from different sources. All traditions have a common foundation for which each of us can find evidence in himself, provided he submits to suitable preparation. The dominant purpose of our teaching is to unify life, and its fundamental character is to form a living unity. Such teaching is a living whole on every plane of life and finds more complete expression in a living community than in a book. That is why one cannot pick and choose from it without dismembering it and putting it to death.

By what sign will you be able to tell whether you are called by this teaching rather than another?

If, as you read, you say to yourself: *But I know all that!*, you will be right, for here are clear and simple things that go without saying, and each of us should be right in thinking he knows them. You will also be right in thinking you should seek elsewhere.

If, on the contrary, you say: *This is strange stuff! I've never heard anything like it before!*, you will be understating the facts. You ought to say: *This is outrageous! It turns everything upside down!* Be that as it may, it is not for you.

But if, as you read these pages, you seem to be following your own thoughts; if this book speaks to you with your inner voice; if you not only understand these things but know them for your own, and are nevertheless struck by them as by something quite new; if they not only give you a feeling of newness, but also the feeling that you have been renewed, THERE IS THE SIGN, and you are called.

So come and take, give and do!

# KNOWLEDGE AND POSSESSION
# OF THE SELF

The predominant attitude in this world is one of self-ignorance, that is, a state of forgetfulness of the soul, or inattention, constant indifference, the turning of the mind toward profit, and a claiming and attempt to dominate the outside world, both people and things.

Conversion (or the reversal of what sin has reversed, in other words, setting upright again) consists in coming out of the world, coming out of the outside, coming back into oneself. Above all, paying attention to that self.

Illuminated by the ray of attention, the vague and insubstantial soul becomes alive and aware, a source of original and significant words and deeds. Self-knowledge is unifying and radiant, unlike knowledge of other things, since knowledge of any outer thing has absolutely no effect on that thing.

The hunger to possess things and subjugate other people has its counterpart in the inability to possess and control oneself.

If self-knowledge is lucid and even illuminating, but passive and without strength, there can be no self-fulfillment. True knowledge of the true self is shown by the majesty of the radiating center, its power to bring order and peace into the whole person, including his instincts and bodily functions. Its natural result is detachment from worldly goods and respect for the freedom of others. That is why the Gospel says, "Blessed are the poor in spirit for theirs is the Kingdom of Heaven." Since they have kingship within them and therefore in the substance, why should they chase after shadows and appearances in the outer darkness and the artificial world of the city of men?

Nevertheless, one can control oneself and yet not give oneself. By strong self-discipline, a man may seek, cultivate, and obtain knowledge and magic power. Whoever is master of himself has overcome the world. But beware of the Prince of This World! One can fall into the hands of the tempter unwittingly. To become the servant of the Devil it is not necessary to use one's powers and gifts for evil. It is enough to cherish them for their own sake and for oneself, to use them for one's own profit, for the very essence of Original Sin is to pluck the fruit for oneself. This is the "sin against the spirit."

In a certain sense, of course, self-possession must precede self-giving, for one cannot give what one does not have. But the self should be possessed solely in order to give. Dispossession should never be absent from all our efforts to acquire self-possession.

In the spiritual exercises we do, relaxation is constantly kept in mind as the bodily reflection of this truth.

At every step in our exercises, the attitude of release is combined with its opposite. Like all effort, spiritual effort is accompanied by tension, which fortifies and unites the center, hardens it, and separates it from the rest. Death will ensue if the tension is not accompanied by relaxation, a readiness to give and to receive.

At the height of the struggle and in the moment of victory, let there be serenity, indifference to the result, humility. "Yet not I labored," says St. Paul, "but the Grace of God which was with me." Self-effacement and strength, renunciation and transcendence, sacrifice and joy will be found together.

I shall not speak of the doctrine of Buddah. His statue speaks for itself. A man seated. His face is as blank and smooth as an egg, his limbs flow like loose ribbons or water, his hands flower, his feet flower, his chest flowers, his hair is like a flower, his smile scarcely perceptible. There is nothing here that is not given, given up, given back. But go round and look at his back. It is a wall, unshakable on its foundations, upright and straight, the strength and height from which his gentleness flows.

## LYING

It is true that by means of small lies one sometimes avoids great trouble and that if one did not lie a little, life would become difficult.

But if one told no lies, sin would become impossible and all the disgrace in the world would dry in the sun.

## HELPING OTHERS

Do not help others.

It would be trying to do more than God who lets them struggle and sin at ease.

Help them to help themselves.

## THE STRAIT GATE

*. . . strait is the gate and narrow is the way which leadeth unto life, and few there be that find it. (Matt. 7:13)*

Not unreasonably, this is usually understood to mean that the road to ruin is a smooth one. But there is more to it than that. Nowhere is it said, "Take the rough road." *Strait* means narrow. We feel that it must be a hard road, and steep, but there is a further meaning. This road is the one that goes *the other way*, the road inward, through the narrow gate.

What can be narrower than the One? And what can be more difficult to reach and enter than the central point? There is no space in a point, no space in inner life, and inner life begins by being a sort of strangling, a difficult passage through the mouth of a well. You can only get through if you are simple enough, small enough, and naked, free of everything you were attached to, all the things that encumbered you or swelled you up and prevented you from passing. The road is difficult, not because of its roughness or its steepness, but because of its narrowness. Only the simple and the naked can get through.

And perhaps the road does not go up, but down. Down into the well.

## ETERNAL TRUTH

How can something eternal be new?

Whenever something eternal is affirmed, it appears in the lightning flash of absolute newness. It startles us. But unlike an ordinary surprise which, as soon as one is used to it, no longer startles and so ceases to be a surprise, the newness of eternal things strikes us ever more deeply as we enter into them and they enter us.

# THE VIRTUE OF SILENCE

Even when it is the truth that is speaking through us, we must sometimes be wise enough to keep silent. Throughout the ages, the wise, and Jesus Christ foremost among them, have warned us to keep quiet and hide, to keep the best in us silent and hidden lest we "have our reward" in showing it off. But also for fear of other dangers. In all ages but ours, the wise went to great lengths in their observance of secrecy. They had four, or rather five, main reasons for doing so.

The first is that knowledge is power and that it is not fitting to put power into the hands of the unworthy. This is what Jesus makes clear when he says, "Lest the swine turn on you and rend you." If you have a pistol, it is not right to put it into the hands of a raging madman. If you have a razor, it is not right to put it into the hands of a chimpanzee running wild in a house full of children lest the chimpanzee, like his civilized brother, cut the throats of everybody in the house, including himself. For this obvious reason, the great secrets of science have been kept hidden with the utmost care until this very day; hidden by the Egyptian priests who had studied and learned them, hidden by the sages of China and their wise emperors, hidden even in empires as evil and rotten with vice as was the Roman Empire.

It was not until the insanity of today that science was allowed (with what complacency, with what irresponsibility and criminal foolishness!) to spread destruction and yield its deadly fruit. The alchemists of the Middle Ages, in daily contact with the formidable forces of nature, knew them thoroughly, probably much better than the chemists of today, but took jealous care to keep silent about them. A technical secret was guarded under pain of death and transmitted only to tried and trustworthy apprentices. Only in a secret code were the results of experiments recorded, and these astonishing records are still coming to light.

The sages knew that knowledge is a blessing only if all the virtues of its possessor are in harmony with it. They knew that bulky, bulging, flashy knowledge crammed into a base or imperfectly purified nature, far from being a blessing, is a total evil. Before a truth could be transmitted (and here I am speaking of merely external and natural truth), the character of the receiver had to be tempered and illuminated. He had to have decided what end he was pursuing, and confirmed the good intent of his pursuit; he had to have proved himself completely disinterested. Then and then only could he gradually be entrusted with the pearls of wisdom, the ultimate particle, living gold, the philosopher's stone, the stone of transmutation, the principle of inner change, so that light might dawn on his spirit and his heart might render thanks to God. But not so that he might sell these secrets to big companies and armies in exchange for money, medals, and honorific titles.

The second reason for hiding what one knows is that knowing is a manner of being born, of coming to life, and all life is hidden. There is no creature alive, not even a fly, that does not hide and keep secret the principle that makes it live. If you open a seed, it dries. If you open a lizard, it dies. If truth is to be living truth, its center must be deep, hidden, or contained in a form which alone appears. Truth itself does not appear. The more precious and profound a truth is, the more secret and sacred it must be held. Therefore religions have never explained the object of worship, have never exposed it but only revealed it, that is to say, shown it under a luminous veil. What is most brilliant, most luminous, Light itself, God Himself, is also what is darkest, most awesomely secret and hidden. In consequence, the name of God in four letters (the Hebrew letters ɪʜᴠʜ) could not be given profane or untimely utterance because of spiritual modesty, without which there can only be vulgarity and blasphemy.

The third reason for keeping silent is respect for the dignity of knowledge, since knowledge is given to man, and every perversion of this divine power, this divine light, is not just one of a number of sins, it is The Sin, the biting of the fruit, the biting into the Fruit of Knowledge. Respect for the dignity of knowledge makes it a sacrilege to turn knowledge upside down, sacrilege to pursue an end that flouts the very reason for knowledge. It is criminal, monstrous (and all who wittingly or unwittingly devote themselves to the disgraceful task will be punished), monstrous that knowledge should be employed for utility. It is disgusting that it should be used by man to evade the laws of the human condition, for he must earn his bread in the sweat of his brow and not cheat in this respect, but prepare and achieve his redemption, at least in part, by hard work. It is disgusting and outrageous that knowledge should be used for making machines, whereas knowledge was given us so that we should acquire the opposite of the machine: conscience. And all who give themselves up to the hellish task will be destroyed and indeed already are. It is monstrous that knowledge, divine knowledge, should be employed by man in order to make the bestial part of himself triumph and serve his appetites (and if it were only his appetites!). For he also perverts knowledge to serve his artificial desires. It is monstrous that the human beast should triumph by his intelligence so that it becomes an affliction for all creatures. In ancient times, to practice mathematics and physics as we do was held an abomination. Mathematics to Plato meant the contemplation of numbers, and mathematical speculation was a spiritual exercise just as it is for the Hindus, for whom it consists in contemplation of the *yantra* or geometrical form which symbolizes the attributes of divinity and represents the facets of supreme unity. It is not a science of calculation: it is not for the use of the merchant or the gunner or the technician.

A further reason for hiding and keeping silent is that whoever is seeking for truth loves truth, and whoever loves abstains from making a vulgar show of the object of his love. He abstains from cutting it up, from taking it to bits and putting it together again for sport or in the hope of gain. He wants the object of his love to be clad in beauty. Accordingly, the knowledge of the sages and the profound wisdom of religions has always been expressed in symbols, in poems and songs of a beauty totally incomparable with that of songs made only for the sake of beauty. You cannot, if you have any pity for the weakness of human nature, compare the Bible or the *Upanishads* or the Egyptian *Book of the Dead* or the Gospels with even the greatest masterpiece a great artist has ever composed to please or move us. Only the sacred books can so overwhelm us with beauty. Of them alone can it be said that "Beauty is the splendor of truth."

The last and fifth reason for keeping silent and hiding the truth, or at least for keeping it hidden for a long time while letting it be felt that one could and would like to reveal it, is that truth is the most precious thing there is, and whoever would acquire it must suffer in order to feel and savor its worth. He must make great efforts to attain it, can only approach it by climbing step by step, must sweat blood and tears to reach and enter it, must be ready to give and give up all he has. So it is kinder, if you have a truth to teach someone, not to throw it in his face at the very outset. In any case, he would not understand. You can hold up a lighted candle, it will never give light to the blind, and we all live blindly. Blind to the invisible light. And our blindness to it is not an unjust affliction visited upon us by Heaven. Even if our blindness is not voluntary, it is always, up to a certain point, a lack of will to see clearly. Only when natural man, that is to say, blind man has acquired and developed the will to see clearly can his inner clarity grow, and his will to see clearly must be aroused by revealing or hiding the truth as befits his case.

We have seen for what reasons the sages were silent, and what the principal good reasons are for keeping silent; but there are also bad ones. The text (Matt. 5:14) continues, "For everyone that doeth evil hateth light, neither cometh to the light, lest his deeds should be reproved." And this applies to lying and ignorance which are, moreover, one and the same thing as evil. Ignorance also hides, and cunning ignorance, scheming stupidity employs the same methods to hide its ignorance as the sages to hide their knowledge. Thus the charlatan and the false prophet surround themselves with spectacular mystery and have the art of saying and not saying, and sometimes show themselves and sometimes hide, and all their entries, their exits, and their poses are carefully staged.

Furthermore, sharing a secret is a real possibility of union, and from union power is generated which may be profitable to the possessor of the secret. So it may be in the interest of a rogue to feign a secret that does not exist, in order to gain the support of dupes or accomplices, or half-dupes and half-accomplices, who will keep the secret and the oath of secrecy, and thanks to this fraternity, develop questionable power. That is how the secret societies which still infect our civilization have spread and been perpetuated, if not founded. It also happens that through guarding the secret, through taking precautions to leave no recognizable trace of it, those who are supposed to know it end up by forgetting it.

If it is true that Freemasons are the direct descendants of the builders of the cathedrals (which has not been proved and cannot be proved), then they must have possessed secrets, venerable secrets which were doubtless at the origin of their power, for which mere fraud could not account. But, God knows how, perhaps simply by excessive secrecy, their knowledge has gradually been lost. When one learns that the so-called philosopher Voltaire was initiated and received his apron from the hands of Helvetius, and if one knows any of the petty politicians who have pride of place in these mysterious associations and have gone through more or less Egyptian initiations of some sort, one point appears certain: Freemasons are not in the secret of things.

The problem therefore arises, and always will arise, of how open one should be, how secret one should be. To what extent is preaching vulgarization and vulgarity? To what degree is it martyrdom, that is to say, testimony to the truth? In what form should truth be taught, and to whom, and at what moment? And should it be taught in one way to some and in another way to others? Should one person teach it one way, and another differently? Are not both perhaps affirming the same truth on different planes in spite of their dissimilar and even contradictory forms of expression?

To this question, I feel an answer is given by the texts we are now studying, as well as by the example of the Church. The Gospel is accessible to all. One can hear it any day at any hour of the day, and it seems childishly clear and simple. But which of us is child enough to understand it? It shines out like a lighted candle, but only those who have eyes to see can see. And however much it is read and preached, its meaning, like the meaning of every living thing, guards itself from those who have no ears to hear.

As for the Church, like all great schools of wisdom, it offers a catechism and a moral code to all and sundry, but it has its theology and its secret language, Latin, and very wisely forbids the reading of the Bible profanely, without a commentary; and although it makes public its ceremonies with all their astonishing, admirable, and ageless symbols, it explains them to nobody. "He that hath eyes to see, let him see, and he that hath ears to hear, let him hear!" Many are called, but few are chosen.

For there is a barrier the profane cannot surmount. Jesus proclaims it clearly to the crowds who follow Him. "Unless you hate your father and mother, your children, your very life, unless you take up your cross, you cannot be my disciple." But if you are happy to be persecuted, happy to be broken-hearted, happy to be poor in spirit and hungry for the spirit of love of the spirit, if your heart is pure, that is to say, purified by long search for the light, the terrible separations and detachment that will be demanded of you before you are clad in raiment of light, then you will see God, and you will be able to make your good works manifest without vainglory, for they will not glorify you, but God. As for you, you will enter glory when you die. You will go into glory living.

# ORIGINAL ERROR

We carry this error* in us. It is the burden that makes us fall into darkness. There is no escape from it until we reach old age, until the time comes when the Spirit awakens. The child at the breast cannot conceive of himself otherwise than as a body.

Not without reason, then, do we call error *original*† since it lies in our origin, is common to us all, is ours at birth.

But how can we admit our error and still err? When a man is mistaken, he does not know that he is mistaken, or, as soon as he finds out that he is, he ceases to be mistaken.

That is true where all other error is concerned, but original error is too deeply rooted in our nature. Certainly if, like the common man, we are unaware of our common error, we cannot find or even look for the way out. Knowing we err in this way does not put an end to our error, but enables us to seek a remedy. If I know, then my head is above water, which is already a great deal, for I can breathe. But the rest of my body is still steeped in error.

In no court is ignorance of the law an excuse. Likewise, no one has the right to be ignorant of truth, and no one who is ignorant of it can go scot-free. There is no innocence in such ignorance. It is not an excuse for sin, but sin itself. And we give it the name of original error so as to connect it with the sin of the same name, an offense against the Tree of Knowledge.

* Error concerning the self.
† *Original error* reminds us of *Original Sin*, an aspect of which it undoubtedly is.

# THE PERSON AND THE PERSONAGE

The catechism teaches us that man is a creature formed of a body and a soul. However, body and soul present themselves to us as a person.

You know what a body is, or at least you think you do. I think you don't, and it would be foolishness on my part to say that I know, for to know what the body is would be to possess all the secrets of nature. I am not one of those who despise the body. I believe that the body is the plumb line that fathoms the whole of creation, its measure and its key, since the body is the only object in the world that we experience from the outside and the inside at the same time. It is therefore the way by which we can enter the inside of everything.

But it is not of the body that I want to speak now. I shall not speak of the soul either, neither of its nature nor its unity nor its immortality. It is of the person I want to speak today, of the person, or rather, the personage. For by the word *person* we understand two quite distinct things. Person means a part acted in a play. Person also means the flowering of the spiritual substance. It is in this second sense that theologians say that God is made of Three Persons. But where the human person is concerned, it is nearly always the word *personage* that applies.

Every man, then, not only possesses a body and a soul, he also possesses—or rather, since his mastery of it is doubtful, he has—a personage. Nevertheless, the catechism is right, in my opinion, to omit any mention of this important part of man when speaking of him as one of God's creatures, because God did not create this image. The body, as a natural being, is one of God's creatures; the soul, as a spiritual being, is one of God's creatures; but the personage, which falls between the two, is a creature of man, a social fiction. It is a composition, not an element: a passage, not a being.

The first thing to note when one is studying a personage is its unreality. The personage is a manufactured being, more or less hollow and false. It is not born with the person but manufactured little by little in the course of his upbringing. This manufacturing continues through his schooldays, his selective service, his college career or employment in a factory, his home and social life, and all his dealings, pleasant or unpleasant, with other people.

Education, culture, law, and custom, which are all artifices, contribute to it. Language is an artifice, one of the greatest. The very existence of the personage is not only confirmed, but almost created by the name others give it, the reputation they attribute to it and the "Personally, I . . . " it attributes to itself.

The leaven of the personage, the yeast that makes it swell, is vanity. The vacuum at its center sucks in the substances of the two poles, which mingle there. Vanity is the wind that inflates the personage and drives it forward in life, makes it gesticulate and take up as much space as possible until it comes up against the vanity of the personages around it, who deflate it and put it back in its place.

If the word *persona* means the part played by an actor on a stage, it is natural that the personage should above all be a mask, a theatrical costume and, even, a puppet. Well may we wonder what reason for existence this strange nonexistent thing has and what we are to do with it.

Empty and unreal though it be, it is nevertheless indispensable. Indeed, there are two reasons, or rather, three, for the existence of the personage. These are: action on others, self-expression, and protection of the natural man. What *can* we, what *are* we to do with it? We should be mistaken in thinking it easy to find a use for it or to suppose that, for all its vanity and nonexistence, it cannot withstand our endeavors. In all human affairs, nothing is easier than to take the means for the end and to stop halfway, and this is just what people who mistake their personage for themselves do. Let us not deceive ourselves: they are the great majority of cultured men, of persons who do not purely and simply take themselves for their bodies. Man is the dupe in this authorless comedy in which the personage is his role. He plays the part and does not know that he is playing a part. He plays and thinks he is doing. He represents and thinks that he is, and his puffed-up, empty, faked, and imaginary image absorbs all the strength of his being.

I think we can safely say that the object of education, morality, and culture is to produce persons. Years of study and training by demanding teachers, good manners, schools, libraries, the theater, sport, social intercourse, travel, learning, as well as natural gifts and ability and charm, opportunity, and all the civilization these imply are necessary, but not always sufficient, for their formation.

In the eyes of the world, nothing is more admired, loved, and envied than an accomplished person. Success, honor, happiness, fortune, and glory are his natural due. What can be the reason for such prestige in everyone's eyes?

This is the reason: *his spiritual nature is clad to perfection. And we should know that the soul cannot appear in society naked any more than the body can.* First, for the excellent reason that the soul is invisible. It can only appear clad in the person. The body clothes itself in order to hide; the soul clothes itself in order to appear. Moreover, the clothing of the one and of the other overlaps, for the body's clothing insofar as it is representative and significant, is one of the manifestations that make up the person.

But why clothing? Why this decorative lie? What does this representation represent?

Since clothing of the body is universal among mankind, there is a reason for it, and beyond all doubt, that reason is religious.

It is all very well to declare that the pompous apparel so-and-so glories in serves to conceal a creature rather like a worm; reducing him to the nakedness of a worm would be giving him even more false a form than do the artifices that adorn him. For man is less than he claims to be but more than he appears. He therefore clothes himself in the signs of what he aims at being, and with them covers the reality of his appearance: his nakedness. As soon as he dresses and adorns himself, he puts himself on some rung of the social and spiritual hierarchy. He is then no longer his simple self: he represents what he wants to be, can be, must be. And the basic reason for this is not vanity but an immense aspiration toward wholeness of being. The person *is not*, it represents. It does not *lie*, it represents. It represents the truth concerning the nature of man, a dual nature, for man is a path and a possibility.

By representing, man sets his course. He does not reveal his form, but shows in what direction lies the form to which he aspires. Representing is not a purely lyrical activity. It is effective magic, a religious obligation, a spiritual exercise, and the first of all duties.

Indeed, there can be no direction and no transformation for man if he has not fixed his aim, or if that aim is void of being and form, or if he does not keep his aim, its being, and form constantly in mind.

His aim, its being, and form are divinity.

Keeping his aim present is presenting himself to it by sacrifice and prayer and representing it, that is to say, recalling it and reproducing its form. It is conforming to it by imitating and incorporating it, *clothing himself in its form.*

The feast, the holy day or holiday, is the periodical return of representation. Ceremony is the properly religious—in other words, obligatory—form of representation. It is accompanied by other, freer kinds, more inward and more exalting, such as the sacred dances and plays in which the actor wears the guise and mask of the God, becomes possessed by the God's breath and drunk with His strength, speaks with His voice and for a moment is He.

But there are men who act this role permanently. They are the Priest and the King (in the beginning, one and the same).

At the summit and center of the people, they represent divinity, and all their life is feast, rite, and ceremony; that is to say, not wealth and pleasure, but representation.

Now the King is represented by the lord in his domain, by the captain in his army, by the teacher in his school, by the master in his workshop, by the father in his family, and even by the humblest of free men in that a free man is master of his body and lord of his own life, and possesses a spark of royal majesty, a reflection of the divine light. And that spark of majesty, that glint of divinity is the Person.

And here we see the person we first presented as eminently frivolous and false in a new light, and here we have new indications of how we should behave toward it. For the person can be divine, diabolical, or vain. It becomes diabolical as soon as a man believes in it, as soon as he believes in his own person. I mean that instead of using it as a representation of the aim, he makes it the aim itself, the center and the God it should tend toward. Then the King turns into a tyrant and the man becomes a demon. Representation becomes lying, dignity becomes pride, and man does what Satan did before him, Satan who was Lucifer, *the bearer of light*, and took himself for the Light, for which he was cast headlong down.

But when, on the contrary, man attaches no importance or significance to his person, then the person is no longer demonic or monstrous, but insignificant. This is nearly always the case in what is known as "society." The persons there are what they can be. Their friendliness does not spring from friendship, their sensitivity is self-indulgence, and they have no aim since they are self-centered and their selves are nothing.

What purpose does the person serve? It is a sign. It should be a reminder of human dignity to all other men. We should respect it in ourselves only for this reason. Because of its purpose, we should never humiliate it in ourselves or in others, since it is a reminder and a representation of Godhead. Only for this must it be respected, and when it knowingly gives the soul its clothing of truth, venerated.

Persons are rare in this world, and precious. If you chance to meet a person, don't let him go without trying to make a friend of him. Friendships are made between persons. A person is a man who creates a work of art of the personage I was talking about; who uses his person to communicate with other men and express himself; who accomplishes the very difficult and delicate task of composing his person from expressions he has learned and attitudes he has imitated. He borrows these things from outside, chooses and arranges them tastefully, and from elements as artificial and common to us all as language, manners, and dress, succeeds in making a whole which is beautiful, balanced, original, and of worth.

You must nevertheless know that the tragedy of the person, whatever its dignity and the perfection it attains, is that it must die, die moreover without leaving a trace behind; and also, that it is right that it should die. The body, as you know, dies and rots, yet it is inhabited by a formal substance which does not die but is summoned at the Resurrection.

The person has no substance and consequently falls aside like a cast-off garment. The body is sometimes said to be a rag. It is not a rag, but the person is. And all the trouble men take to compose an admirable "image" and leave in men's minds a memory of its glory is labor lost.

Let us remember God and take care of our souls and let the person grow spontaneously from within. We shall then have no need to put together a masterpiece that in the end would crumble and disappoint all our hopes.

Wisdom, like simple good manners, has always taught that the person should efface itself. The Gospel says, "If any man desire to be first, the same shall be last of all, and servant of all." Gandhi, like so many others before him, observed: "Whoever wants to approach God must reduce himself to nothing." Mystics of all times have cried, "I am nothing!" and if *I* means my person it is neither a figure of speech nor passionate exaggeration, but an exact metaphysical statement.

"But," you may object, "are not the saints *persons* and even holy *images?*"

Yes, indeed, and compared with heroes of novels, tragedy,

or epics, they are more striking and more singular. But that is not because they have affirmed or developed their persons, or cultivated, educated, adorned, or exalted them. On the contrary, it is because they have emptied them. For not only shall the first be last, but "There are last which shall be first."

Whoever puffs himself up shall be found empty, but whoever empties himself shall be filled. When man ceases venting his good or bad temper, showing off his little or great talents, hoping for fortune or glory thanks to his learning and acquired abilities, the Holy Ghost will have room to inspire him, to sound through him and send out its call.* And if the role of the person is to signify that which surpasses it, here is glorious fulfillment: the person becomes a spirit.

## LOOK WITHIN

If thoughtlessness is a disease of this spirit, how can one cure oneself of it, unless by attention, inward attention?

But when I close my eyes and turn my sight inwards, what do I see? Nothing. The dark. So I feel afraid, or bored, or run away from myself.

Yes, but wait! Have you ever happened to go into a cellar from a sunny yard? What do you see in the cellar? Darkness. No, not even darkness: a dazzle of gnatlike sparks dancing in front of your eyes. And how long will it take you to see in the dark? Twenty minutes. And if there is treasure in the cave, how long will it take you to see it gleaming? An hour.

---

* A possible etymology of *persona*: *sonare*—to sound, *per*—through. The person? That through which a meaning sounds. God grant that it be true!

But which of you has remained for a whole hour steadily gazing at the dark within?

Try it and you will see!

I am not going to tell you what you will see and I am not asking you to believe me. I am not asking you to believe what you have heard or read about it. I am asking you to go and see for yourself and come back and tell me what you have seen.

Certainly, staying alone with oneself for a whole hour looking into one's inner darkness cannot be the first step. It is too difficult. It has to be approached gradually. The first step will be to brave the contrary current of attachment, the contrary wind of letting oneself be carried away, the winds of dispersion or total dissipation, the state of nonbeing.

If one is scattered, involved in too many things at once, it is as if one were not. The first exercise we recommend to you, busy friend, you who have so many important things to do and so little time, will not take you an hour, half an hour, or even a quarter of an hour, but three minutes, and where is the man so pressed for time that he does not take three minutes to wash his hands? And perhaps three minutes is still too much, so let us divide them into six: six times a day, three times in the morning, and three times in the afternoon, be still. Stop!

You are in a hurry? All the more reason for checking yourself. You have things to do? Stop, otherwise you will make mistakes. You have to look after other people? All the more reason for beginning with yourself, lest you harm those others.

So, unharness. Relax. For half a minute every two hours, stop! Put down what you have in your hand. Hold yourself straight. Breathe deeply. Draw your senses inward. Suspend yourself before the inner dark, the inner void. And even if nothing happens, you will have broken the chain of haste. Say to yourself, *I am recalling myself, I am taking myself back*. That is all. Say it to yourself, but above all, do it. Recollect yourself, as the words say so strongly. To recollect oneself is to gather up all the shreds of oneself that were dispersed and clinging to things here and there. Answer as Abraham answered God's call: "Present" (*Adsum!*).

The exercise consists, then, in remaining present to oneself and to God for half a minute.

Suspended at the mouth of the inner well.

It is unlikely that in so short a time you will plunge deeply into the mystery of self, but it is not impossible with the grace of God. However, even if nothing else happens during the moment of suspension, we shall at least have broken the chain of events that held us prisoner. We shall have broken it in six and taken the first step toward deliverance. Besides, if we want not only to recall ourselves to awareness, but also to remember to recall ourselves every two hours, we shall have to practice latent and continuous remembrance throughout all the actions and thoughts of our waking day.

Recall, or self-recollection, is the first step toward self-knowledge, or awareness.

## LOVE THY NEIGHBOR AS THYSELF

We spend our lives turning our backs upon ourselves. We have eyes, thoughts, and feelings only for other things.

How could I know, how could I love someone on whom I always turn my back?

Come now! You're not going to tell me that people sin through lack of self-interest and because they love other people too much?

No, I didn't say that. What I am talking about is their indifference and their heedlessness. They are quite incapable of loving their neighbors like themselves since they do not love themselves.

And selfish people! Are you going to tell me that they don't exist or that they are few and far between?

No, but I say that they do not love themselves at all, and I shall prove it to you if you lend me one. I shall take this selfish person who, you say, loves himself so much, and put him in a dark room and shut him in. Now, what could be more delightful than to be shut up in a dark room with someone you love? But just listen to him! What's wrong with him? Why is he shouting like that? Shouting for help as if he had fallen into a ravine, banging on the door with his two fists as if he were trying to escape from some wild beast, yelling with horror as if he had seen a ghost, screaming as if he were being tortured?

Do you need further proof that he cannot bear himself, cannot bear to be alone with himself for one single moment? Actually, you will always see our egoist busy with other people, clinging to them with all his strength and all his weight because he needs them to occupy him, to amuse and entertain him, to while away his boredom, to use for any purpose they may serve, but above all to avoid having to face the dullest and dourest of all the people he has no time for: himself.

But unless you yourself are an idiot, you will never call a solitary an egoist.

Have you ever seen a man who loves himself? There are not many. You have heard *Love thy neighbor* preached.

Have you ever heard *Love thyself?* Have you been taught this truth, that it is the first of your duties? *Thou shalt love thy neighbor as thyself* is what is said. But if you do not love yourself, how can you love your neighbor?

*As thyself*, it says. Let us insist on the *as*.

*As* means *in the same manner* and *as* means *in the same measure*. Which means neither more nor less, nor less nor more. And there are two sins of love: *less* and *more*.

Woe unto him who loves another more than himself! It would be a mistake to think this rare. The passionate and the perverted all do so. They love others more than they love themselves. They even love their own destruction. They love the loss of themselves. They love their destroyer. The object, with all its limits, or the person with all its limits as an object, is loved and adored as an absolute.

Which is the beginning of the darkest passions. "For each man kills the thing he loves," said someone who knew a lot about this kind of love. And each man kills himself in this kind of love.

Now, I must draw your attention to the fact that never does it happen that a man is smitten with passion for bread or milk. Why? Because bread is a good thing. Because milk is a good thing. When you have eaten your fill of bread, it's finished. You stop. When you have drunk a glass of creamy milk, you don't want any more. You *can't* drink any more. But when you love a thing passionately, the thing must be a poison or a drug, or a woman who serves as a poison or a drug. And when you stop kissing her, it is to fight with her. Until one day, you strangle her and hang yourself for lack of love of yourself.

Where is he to be found, the man who loves himself, who loves his integrity, his fulfillment, and salvation? What people love is their pleasure, their ease, their success. They love everything in themselves except themselves.

*Themselves.* Let us look at the word. *Self* means *same.* Which reminds us of Plato's great theme. The *Self* and the *Other* are for Plato the two faces of the world, the reverse and obverse of each other, like what we have called the inside and the outside. The self is the same everywhere. It is the other that separates and is separate. Myself, yourself, himself: self is the same for all three.

When a man speaks well, listen to what he says, but above all, let his words speak in you, for they mean more than the speaker means. Listen to their echoes and their meanings. In their sound, something remains of the original revelation deposited in them before Babel. It is not always necessary to learn philology to understand them, it is enough to learn to be silent. Just as through fasting we can catch a glimpse of the terrible mystery of food and through vigil, of the consoling mystery of sleep, so through silence the attentive enter the depths of the word, and through the word, the secret of things.

"It is not for love of one's friend that one loves one's friend, nor for love of one's spouse that one loves one's spouse, nor for love of one's son that one loves one's son, but for love of the Self." And the careless translator of the *Upanishad* has written "But for love of oneself," so that the door is open to foolish speculation and discussion of Eastern wisdom and how little importance it attaches to love, whereas what is meant is the pure charity the Gospel teaches with even greater force: "If any man come to me, and hate not his father, and mother, and wife, and children, and brethren, and sisters, yea, and his own life also, he cannot be my disciple" (Luke 14:26); and, "Thou shalt love thy neighbor as thyself." For one loves one's neighbor, not for his charm as Other, nor out of attachment to one-self, but for love of God.

Now there is Other in me, and Self in others. Loving is recognizing oneself in others by grace of the Self.

In yourself and your neighbor you shall hate Other. In others and in yourself, you shall love the Self.

The cause of all evil is that Self and Other are everywhere mixed, except in God who is One, Unique, and the Same. Distinguishing them is knowing clearly and loving purely.

The Self or Same is therefore in itself love, and every sin against it is a sin against love.

## ONE-POINTEDNESS

While the landscape unfolds and your feet and knees work away under you, keep your heart steady, sharpen your mind to pointedness, and endeavor to bring that pointedness to bear on one point.

## THE MUSTARD SEED

The third parable is that of the mustard seed. The Word is no longer compared to a grain of wheat, the grain that nourishes, but to an exciting, spicy seed. And it is said that this seed is the tiniest of all, yet it will grow into one of the greatest of herbs and become a tree, so that the birds of the air will come and lodge in its branches.

This parable underlines the secrecy and mystery of the flowering of the Word. Secret, because although truth is in us from our birth, the singular thing about it is that we do not know it and hardly think about it. Therefore it is a seed, but almost imperceptible. It is the most vigorous, the most spicy and joyful, but the least of seeds, because our attention is turned from it by the flavor and size of outer things. It is secret because it is alive; full of hidden worth because it is alive. It is more important than mountains that are huge, have always been huge, and will remain so until little by little wind and rain wear them away. It is even more important than the stars it resembles, but in whose mighty, luminous mass there is perhaps not a spark of the essence called life and awareness.

## ATTENTION

All work is useless for the salvation of the soul until the day of conversion.

And conversion begins by turning the attention the other way, by focusing it on the Self.

Let there be no misunderstanding. There is no question here of understanding impulses, motives, or complexes, but of seizing the Self as a pure and simple inner unity.

This hub, this kernel, this center, this point "smaller in the heart than the germ in a grain of millet, bigger than all these worlds" (Shandilya), this secret hearth, this den of darkness, this tight knot is the strait gate and the narrow path to initiation, and inner attention is the first step on that path.

That is the reason for recall.

Recall should be practiced in its three forms: the interrogative form, the negative form, and the affirmative form.

Interrogative recall consists in asking yourself, every time you say "I," *Who is* "I"?

Negative recall consists in saying to yourself, *I am not my body, I am not my "image," I am not the thought in my mind at the moment.*

Affirmative recall consists in saying to yourself, *I am re-calling myself* every time you can, every time you remember to do so. For a few moments, you leave whatever you are occupied with, whether it be work or worry or talk or thoughts or any other thing. You withdraw from it and recollect yourself, go back into yourself, plunge for an instant into your inner depths.

Do it at least three times during the forenoon and three times in the afternoon and evening, and as it becomes easier to do, do it more often.

And now I am going to tell you about what I call *a perpetual exercise.*

This is the name I give to an exercise one can do in any circumstances and which neither suspends nor deviates the habitual course of one's daily actions. It can be done at any time, therefore you can devote all your time to it.

It is the exercise of double attention or redoubled attention.

It consists in concentrating your attention on yourself in action.

Not just paying attention to the object, to the purpose, to your work, but to yourself seeing the object, yourself going toward the goal, yourself at work.

Which amounts to relating everything to the inner center and centering yourself in what you are doing.

It is not enough to pay attention to what you are doing.

You must pay attention to yourself doing what you are doing.

This practice incurs no loss of time or energy (on the contrary), no delay, no trouble unless it be during the period of adaptation to a new attitude.

It requires no change in one's occupation or manner, yet the sense, the density, the value of all one's acts are wholly changed.

## UPRIGHTNESS

Uprightness is the direction of man, the imperative sign of his destiny. Uprightness, line and law, column of balance and thrust toward the heights.

Man stands upright. Animals push forward, heads down. Their prey and their purpose lie before them on ground level. Man, upright, stands witness that his end is above and that he is here to be the link between Heaven and earth. Trees also stand upright, but upside down, their mouths buried in the earth, their sex cast into the sky. Only man is upright the right way up. Are we sufficiently aware of this?

The straight line runs right through us. By the vertical line and its movement, one can remove mountains. (This is neither metaphor nor exaggeration.) The mechanics which change the face of the earth so powerfully are largely play on the lever, speculation on the shifting of the vertical.

And this vertical line, so powerful in the outer world, is equally so in the inner. We do not meditate lying down. We do not pray lying down, unless we are ill.

We must feel ourselves inhabited by the upright line, the line of fire. But the fire of life is a fresh green flame, a tree.

The spiritual act accomplished upright reconciles the two opposites, attention and relaxation, watchfulness and peace, *entering sleep wide awake, entering death alive*. This is the spiritual act.

Perfect uprightness is a state of rest. Did you know? Try it and see. Seek for it. Adjust the parts of your body so that they balance on each other. Sway slightly, and when you pass through perfect uprightness, you will feel rest. Look at a ladder carried by two workmen. With great difficulty, they try to set it up and stagger in the effort, but once it is upright it becomes light and they can steady it with a finger. Horses can sleep standing. There is no better or more convenient chair than the one that has no back and forces us to rest on ourselves, for our rest will then be invigorating instead of heavy and degrading. Avoid the orthopedic instruments called armchairs and don't lean on the back of your chair, the upright support is in yourself. Don't lose uprightness when you walk, just move it forward. When you sit down, stay upright from your seat to the back of your head. Remember to recover uprightness if you have lost it while working and you will avoid needless fatigue. The man who carries his uprightness through the day is not precipitated (i.e., thrown head forward). Supported by uprightness, you will see things from a certain distance, you will pause for a moment before answering and if, in addition, you take a deep breath, you will perhaps find something intelligent to say.

There are men from whom a certain majesty emanates. It springs from their possession of uprightness. They radiate peace. One feels safe beside them because they rest on themselves, whereas people and crowds are forever leaning on emptiness and falling over upon one another like wave upon wave.

# RESPECT

*Respect* and *regard* are words which mean looking at. Everything begins with looking, as we know. To respect is to look at with the heart.

The looking of the intelligence is *attention*. The respect due to a person is shown by thoughtfulness or consideration. Both intelligence and a heart are needed for looking, and looking with both eyes, the right and the left, gives the object more relief.

Regarding (etymologically, *looking* is guarding; keeping and guarding oneself from). *Regard* implies protection, conservation, and distance.

For seeing, there must be distinction and distance. For love likewise. It takes two to love. *Thou, the first word of love,* say the Egyptians. In muddle, attachment, and mixture, no regard, no clarity is possible. For the same reason, love without respect is just impurity.

The distinction and the distance that regard and respect require are the opposite of division, aversion, and indifference.

In the word *respect* there is also the sense of the Latin word *species*, which besides meaning species means beauty. This brings out more clearly the link between the appearance looked at and the substance, between the perceptible character and being.

*Respect* means regard, or look, but not all looks are respectful, far from it. Some are contemptuous, mocking, and insolent. Respect is the look directed at being.

And respect demands that sometimes the gaze should

be steady, sometimes the eyes should be raised, lowered, or turned away. Modesty, decency, and discretion are the finer forms of respect.

People say, "I have respect only for those who deserve it." This is a confession that they have judged merit or demerit without looking.

Let it be understood that respect is the barest justice due to every human being as such.

This is the profound truth in the fiction, the convention, the compulsory parody called politeness.

As for us, our desire to free ourselves from worldly vanity and accommodating lies should not take the form of snubbing our fellow men or behaving rudely. Let us escape from pretense by restoring the substance of friendship to the show of friendliness, and to marks of respect their value of truth.

The earnest exercise of respect, ceaseless and without exception, should help us to put order into the tangled skeins of our human relations. Relations with the family we happen to have, the people we meet by chance. There are knots tied by our attractions and tangles knotted by our moods, hidden frayed ends, roughly mended bits, moth-eaten coils of custom.

Respect teaches us how to free ourselves from our dear ones without ingratitude or brutality, how to approach our neighbor without giving him offense.

## RHYTHM AND HARMONY

This rule is a sequel to the first two concerning respect.

Next to respect for others and respect for oneself comes respect for things and the order of things.

Put cleanliness and beauty into the surroundings in which you live, receive your friends, and bring up your children. Your home reflects you and in turn reflects upon you.

I have seen places that are lessons in austerity, greatness of soul, and recollection. Others proclaim their futility and pretension, others again are oppressive. From the walls of some there oozes the clammy sweat of suicide.

You say you own no beautiful objects and have no money to buy any: in all probability you have too many objects and too much money. I remember a Brahmin in India who received me in his mud hut: the only furniture was a reed mat, a jar, and an oil lamp in a niche. In Granada, I have seen caves freshly whitewashed and decorated with one shining copper pan; in Sicily, a family living under the beams of their one and only room, which they shared with the donkey. Now, I have visited mansions and abbeys which in their way were decorated as beautifully, but not more beautifully. I have lived in palaces, lofts, and attics, and I don't know which I prefer, provided order and cleanliness, which cost nothing, reign there.

You will tell me that these cost time, and that you haven't any. But this is where the rule becomes imperative: if you have no time, take some. Take your time, put order into it, and discover that there is a time for everything, as Ecclesiastes says.

*To every thing there is a season,*
*And a time to every purpose under the heaven: . . .*
*He hath made every thing beautiful in his time.*
*(Eccles. 3:1, 11)*

The great beauty of religion is that it fixes feast days in their season and alternates the times: the time for glorification and the time for repentance, the time for commemoration, the times for beseeching, awaiting, and hoping, and that all these times are feast days.

So, if you are religious, put order into the works and days of your life, the six days of intense work and the seventh of complete rest, thinking only of God, of others, and yourself. The hours of work when you forbid yourself to think of holidays and the hours of rest when you forbid yourself to think of what is done or not done or still to do, or to worry about tomorrow.

When you come home, stop thinking about your plans and troubles. Don't talk about them, but think of your wife, think of your children.

There is a day for fasting and a day for feasting. Nights of deep sleep and nights of lofty thought.

A *time to weep, and a time to laugh;*
A *time to mourn, and a time to dance.*     (*Eccles.* 3:4)

Don't muddle everything by untimely agitation and cogitation.

Above all, don't spend your time regretting time past. That is really wasting time.

Don't undertake anything by your own will alone: ask yourself *if the thing is willed,* if it has come in its own time. Question the circumstances and read the signs.

In the hour of happiness, rejoice: in the hour of disaster, reflect.

If you always think other people are to blame for your failures, you will learn nothing from your tribulations, but whoever can say "I was wrong" can right his course.

It is wrong to rush things and wrong to shilly-shally, wrong to force things and wrong to avoid them. The wise man restrains himself for ten years, then acts like lightning or lets his fruit fall gently when it is ripe.

. . .

Ecclesiastes 33:15 and 42:24 teach us that God created all things in pairs of opposites.

Opposites are formed from each other, and both from the same substance.

The earth has two poles, and man has two poles which are man and woman. Woman was taken out of man, and man is born of woman. And woman has two poles, of which one is the-man-in-her, and man has two, of which one is the-woman-in-him (1 Cor. 11, 12).

Shade is formed from light, and light from shade, and every color is an impulse of shade toward light. Thus life and death and the whole rainbow of joys and sorrows are born of each other.

Everything that walks moves by the alternation of right and left. When the alternation is broken, there comes a fall.

Supreme happiness, goodness and rightness, life itself is that pairs should return to union and travel together on the way.

For those who resemble each other are made to assemble, those who are the same to be a pair, the complementary to complete each other, the various to be put one beside the other like pearls on a string, the extremes to touch, opposites to be reconciled, contraries to meet in the unity of the infinite, all limits surpassed.

But evil and death are pairs separating, complementaries countering each other, distinct planes becoming confused, things out of place colliding, the thread of the various breaking, and the pearls falling into the dust.

The Supreme Philosophy is the doctrine of the conciliation of opposites.* But it reaches full understanding of

* *Conciliato Oppositorum*—Giordano Bruno and Nicolas of Cusa.

opposites only, and does not go beyond the debate between Yes and No, and all its solutions raise new problems, whereas music begins with the solution as soon as it sounds rhythm and a chord.

That is why music is wiser than philosophy.

The whole of the outer world, as God has made it in its relative perfection, rises and falls in rhythm like the waves of the sea, and the law of creation is rhythm.

Between the disorder and agitation of things as seen by our limited understanding and impatient hearts, and the steadfast circle of the One, lies the level of rhythmical rise and fall. Passage from one state to the other is therefore achieved through rhythm.

For this reason, whoever cannot submit to the law of rhythm is a breach in the universe and will himself be broken.

And for the same reason, if you cannot sing and dance, you have little likelihood of knowing how to live.

But if you know how to sing and dance, and yet don't know what you are doing when you are singing and dancing, you are merely a buffoon. What you lack is knowing how to live as you dance and as you sing.

The whirling dervish knows what dancing is, motionless in the midst of his movement, and the Benedictine monk knows what singing is. And each of them knows what it means to live as one sings and dances.

## RELAXATION IN ACTION

The remedy for the loss of half our life and strength is in the art of relaxation.

Good manners teach it to a certain extent. They teach

us to moderate our outbursts, to keep our emotions under control, hold ourselves straight and compose our faces. Usually, we are taught these things for futile, worldly reasons. Nevertheless, their price is above that of rubies, for they are decorum and reserve, and without them, one cannot enter the spiritual world. If we did not learn them in childhood for love of the world, we shall have to submit to them at whatever age we may have reached, for love of God. For nothing coarse or vulgar can pass the threshold of holiness.

To be relaxed during work itself is the very hallmark of mastery in every craft and every art. The master of an art, whether he be porter or poet, knows how to develop his effort in rhythmic cycles, concentrating his effort in the down beat, taking advantage of the up beat to possess himself again in repose, combining ease with strength so that he exalts and renews himself in the course of his work, whereas the apprentice clutches the handle of his tool, breaks the blades, loses his breath, and exhausts himself. The woodcutter lets his ax swing down freely, the laborer keeps time with the swing of his spade, the jeweler pulls his saw and pushes his file with a loose wrist, the swimmer lets the water carry him as it flows back, the skier racing over the snow brings his ankles and knees into play and abandons himself to the slope, the acrobat's face is impassive and at the height of danger, he smiles.

Whoever knows how to use those parts of his being that are needed for a particular purpose, leaving all the rest in reserve so as to be able to call on them when required, is master of himself and master of the art of living.

Whether standing or sitting, he will keep his body in its vertical axis, resting it on its points of balance, so as always to hold himself straight without effort or stiffness.

He will accompany what he has to say with shouting, bursts of laughter, arm-waving, or nods or shakes of the head, only when he deliberately intends to impress or represent, and not because he can't help overflowing and spreading himself like milk boiling over.

## BREATHING

*The spirit of man is the candle of the Lord, searching all the inward parts of the belly. (Prov. 20:27)*

You work eight hours a day or more for your daily bread. When you have earned it, you have to go and buy it, do the cooking, stir the sauces, season them, and, above all, think. Think whether there will be enough, and if it will be varied enough and tasty enough? O Martha! So busy and so full of care! Let us pause a little and try not to eat for three days. What will happen? Nothing to upset you, I can assure you. You may even feel much better, and relieved. Now try to stop breathing for a quarter of an hour, and you will die. What is the lesson? That man lives on air much more than on bread. So how is it that you never stop thinking about food, whereas you never think of breathing. Why indeed? Don't be silly—because it costs nothing, of course.

We are born with our first breath and die with our last.

The word *spirit* has the same root as *respire*. *Inspiration* is the wind from on high that comes in; *expiration* is the sigh that dies outside and falls into outer darkness. Life is a fragile gift of inestimable price put into your hands free, and you, you fools, let it fall, out of sheer stupidity and absence of mind. Your breathing is haphazard, cowardly, and mean. Of your natural capacity you take perhaps half, perhaps only a quarter or even less. Which means that you are losing half of your life, or three-quarters of it, through mere carelessness and sheer ingratitude.

And then of course you will go and see the doctor and tell him pathetically that you feel tired, dizzy, heavy after eating, have a pain here or a growth there . . . and perhaps he will tell you the name of your illness, but neither he nor you will wonder why you are ill. He will not ask you:

(1) how you hold yourself,

(2) how you breathe,

(3) what you eat,

(4) whether you are strained and tense, or kind and serene,

(5) what you do to join with the source of life and resist the weight of death in your body.

Health depends on these five questions. The doctor will not ask them. He will stick a needle into your backside and give you the injection you deserve and you will go off bucked up like a donkey that has just been whipped.

If I were a doctor, I should say to nearly all my clients, "Go for a walk. Yes, go out and get some air! Take the air! Take the air every day before meals and even instead of them from time to time. And don't come back any more!" (I don't know that I should make a fortune.)

Good breathing is strictly dependent on good posture. Whoever slumps from the vertical line has constricted, shallow breathing.

To find out how far off the vertical you are, stand close to a wall. Touch it with your heels, both your shoulders, your head (but don't throw your head back; draw in your chin and place your face in the upright line). Press the hollow of your back to the wall, too. Like that, the bellows is in the proper position and well within your grasp. The thorax is lifted and free to do its work. Have you seen a man stricken by death but still standing? His head hangs forward, his shoulders sag, his chest caves in, his knees bend. If you go through life like that, you are condemned: your shoulders and back weigh on your chest, your chest weighs on your stomach, which weighs on your intestines, and everything sags, everything is heavy and stagnant, everything begins to rot. So you will have recourse to alcohol and stimulants, and to the rot you will add poison. Pleasant poison, it is true, but you will soon have to go to the drugstore to buy unpleasant poison. You would do better to raise your head, otherwise you are going to fall. Fall ill, as they so aptly say.

## FOOD

There is an art of eating well that has nothing to do with "gastronomy." To eat well is to take food that strengthens, refreshes, and leaves the head clear; food that does not bemuse the intelligence, excite, burn, or weigh on the stomach. It means taking the fruits of the earth you are living on when nature offers them; putting as little space and time as possible between the earth and your mouth; preparing them with the least artifice possible; presenting them raw or cooking them over a gentle heat. It means restoring your health and strength first and foremost from the brown bread of the earth, the gray salt of the sea, and olive oil and honey of the sun.

We must know that all food is a remedy or a poison: a perfect doctor should be able to do without medicines and correct every deficiency, every engorgement or fever by the quality, the dose, and combination of the daily meal. This is the first thing we ask of the doctors who are Companions in the community. All their lives, Gandhi and Vinoba sought health in this direction. We ourselves are carrying out the same research. As soon as we have made enough experiments on ourselves to have sufficient certainty, we shall let our friends know, and found health centers.

To eat is not only to absorb a certain bulk of matter, but also to introduce into ourselves certain *spirits*. And for the spirit, too, all food is a remedy or a poison. Knowledge of the spiritual influence of foods has been entirely lost. It was certainly the basis of ancient religious observance. It is good to remember, for example, that pork and potatoes nourish heaviness, brutality, and obscurity, and predispose to blindness, obesity, and cancer; that red, raw meat fosters anger, ferocity, persistent hostility; that eggs and oysters put chastity in great danger, whereas whole cereals give strength and peace, green vegetables and wild herbs, freshness and vivacity, fruit and milk, purity and gentleness.

A meat diet, fermented drinks, and tobacco do not provide the body with vigor, any more than a lash of the whip invigorates a horse, whatever one may think. They obstruct inner life and sap nonviolence at the base.

The glutton does not know any of these things and does not care. But when a man seeks, by eating the smallest amount of the simplest and most judiciously chosen food, to keep up his strength and his balance, his mental liberty and tranquility of soul, at the same time communing with other men and all beings in the blessing of the Lord, he has already conquered gluttony.

Gluttony can therefore be overcome by eating; but on the

whole, this is a negative victory, and always a relative and confused one, for it remains difficult to discern between bodily satisfaction and inner benefit.

There is a less devious, less complicated, less knowing, and much clearer and cleaner way of overcoming it, which is to fast.

Moreover, fasting ensures a positive victory, for not only does it uproot gluttony, it also plants in the heart and flesh a hunger and thirst for righteousness.

Fasting is giving or leaving one's share to one's neighbor.

Fasting is not depriving oneself of food and undergoing hunger courageously, but evacuating all thought of food and all desire for it, and consequently evacuating hunger as well.

The will by which one of the most deeply rooted, obscure, and tenacious desires of the flesh is cut off at the base is quite distinct from all desire and everything that springs from the flesh: it is necessarily a pure will that comes from above.

It would be mistaken to think that such precious results require immense effort, years of training, and exceptional grace. On the contrary, I hold that it is within the power of anyone. People are generally astonished and delighted by the rapidity with which they reach this point, provided they try regularly.

I strongly advise all friends of the Ark to give themselves one complete fast day a week, only drinking water and carrying on their daily work as usual. Perhaps during the first attempts they will occasionally feel weak or dizzy, but they will laugh it off and will soon come to know that this regular purification is as health-giving as it is salutary for the soul. (In the Ark, six-year-olds sometimes undertake a fast of their own will and bear it very cheerfully.)

# SPEECH

We shall first speak of being carried away. Why? Because it is a momentary dizziness. More often than not, a state of artificial excitement not rooted in our deeper needs or habits or in attachment. Being carried away is yielding to rash impulse and all the passion and wildness that turns our heads or makes us lose them, not only in drunkenness or debauchery, but in the course of our daily lives. We are carried away by irritation, haste, desire, pleasure, and even by our generous urges, by indignation, laughter, and pity. We live, and if we live, we act. But true action does not carry us away out of ourselves. The center should not be shaken by our actions or pulled right and left at every instant. Whatever the fury of the wind that waves the branches, the trunk must not quiver or leave its axis, else it will break and fall. Today, let us see how the mere fact of speaking can carry us away.

We must become aware of the importance of speech. From ancient times and throughout the ages, philosophers and legend have attributed a divine origin to speech and languages,* and it is a fact that their advent among men remains mysterious. The great mother languages make a particular claim to divine origin: Sanskrit, Hebrew, Egyptian, and Chinese are looked upon by the peoples whose sacred language they are as having existed before the world did, and having served for its creation. The Bible teaches: "And God said, let there be Light; and there was Light." By speaking, He created. Indeed, no better metaphor has

* Which may be all sorts of unspoken signs and expressions.

been found to express the Second Person of the Trinity than to call him the Word, or Logos, because the relationship between the Second Person and the First is the same as between Word and Thought.

Light reflected is still light. *Lumen de lumine*. But it is by speech that thought is reflected. The word *reflect* has two meanings: the first belongs to the beam of light that strikes a mirror and turns back upon itself; the second, to thought refracted by a sign and turned back upon itself. Thought is not complete unless it returns upon itself; otherwise, it cannot be grasped by its thinker, just as light in the interstellar spaces is not luminous until it encounters something that breaks it and makes it shine.

Actually, you cannot think without speaking. Observe yourself when you are thinking alone and in silence; you never cease speaking, and if you are not speaking a language others can understand, that is merely because you are using personal images and signs. Word and thought are so closely interlinked that in certain languages there is only one word for both, as in Greek, for example *(logos)*.

Speech relates to the essence of things by its logical value. Philosophers of note, such as Aristotle and Descartes, look upon thought as the one irrefutable proof of being. I cannot be mistaken in saying, "I think, therefore I am," for I cannot think that I think without thinking and I cannot think without being. But since on the other hand I cannot think without speaking, speech, thought, and being are necessarily linked within me.

That is how, from the logical character of speech, we proceed to its magical character. For magic is entry into the essence of things by means of signs and the power to work directly on that essence by concentrating on the signs. Speech is a magic tool of the first order.

For the same reason, it is the purest object of religious sacrifice, since it represents the quintessence of things at the same time as the sum of our hopes, desires, and thought. For that reason, prayer is the sacrifice of sacrifices, of greater worth than a holocaust and almost the equivalent of martyrdom.

The poetic value of speech is also due to its magical character. It renders sound, image, movement, emotion, and ideas at one and the same time. Speech is both a cry and a gesture. A cry by its utterance, a gesture by its articulation and the image it conveys. The cry is the spontaneous expression of the subject, the gesture, representation of the form or the direction of the object. Subject and object are thus fused into a whole by speech. Painting and architecture on the one hand, music on the other, meet in speech. They are merely developments of speech.

As for the useful functions of speech, is not the most useful that of uniting us with a human group? It enables us to greet, understand, and encourage one another, for each of us is isolated and to a certain extent in distress. Each of us is

> *An infant crying in the night:*
> *An infant crying for the light:*
> *And with no language but a cry.**

Watch a flock of migrating birds. Their almost continuous calling is the circulation of some feeling that passes from one to the other, gains the whole group and makes it a single body. In the same way, speech is one of the most admirable instruments for understanding and agreement between human beings.

Lastly, speech is currency. It serves our daily needs. It

* Alfred, Lord Tennyson, *In Memoriam.*

informs us of our mutual desires, transmits orders and requests, explains and narrates.

I have spoken briefly of all the functions and values of speech because I want you to reflect on what you are doing when you speak, and to make you aware of how wrong it is to speak for nothing. For speech is truly seed, the seed of thought, seed one has no right to scatter at random.

Speech must serve, or sing, or teach, or enlighten, or act, or pray. Every word that is not used for these purposes is a loss of substance, a grave sin you must acknowledge. Every word used for other purposes fritters you away, does harm around you, wears away other people, is a source of distraction, trouble, and confusion. Many of us let ourselves be carried away by empty talk simply because no one has ever told us that it is a sin. But the Gospel says, "Every idle word that men shall speak, they shall give account thereof in the day of judgment" (Matt. 12:36).

Break yourselves of this sin to start with, since the mere thought of it is enough to cure you. You will reform yourselves in this respect according to the degree of control you have acquired over your thought, which is the aim of the exercises we are doing. With little effort, you will gain spiritual benefit and even worthwhile practical results you did not expect.

I remember a small book of Krishnamurti's, not a work of youth but of childhood, since he wrote it at the age of twelve. It contains all kinds of true and graceful things. I remember this passage: "Before speaking, ask yourself whether what you have to say is true, charitable, and timely." True, first. Am I not rashly asserting something of which I am not sure?

Is it charitable? Whom will it benefit? Even if it is true, have I no right to be silent? Most of the time you say things that are not only untrue, and unjust, but also hurtful and useless.

Is it timely? Or will my speaking raise a problem I cannot solve at the moment, causing confusion in people's minds and anxiety in their hearts? Shall I be casting pearls before swine? Is the listener prepared to hear what I have to say? And above all, are these words, uttered in this company at this moment, not profane and in a way sacrilegious?

I shall add still another precept to Krishnamurti's three: have *I* the right to say what I am about to say, even if it is true, charitable, and timely? Have *I* the authority to speak . this truth and do this good, I whose acts contradict what my lips affirm?

Our explanations should enlighten, and correct our lives, not stir up abstract ideas to play with. What I have just said implies a program of work for each of us. We can begin straight away to be careful of what we say. Little by little, we shall come to control our strongest and deepest instincts, which are less artificial than the foible of speaking to no purpose. But let us begin by what is within our reach.

# HASTE

Beware of haste. Escape from it, fight it, for it is one of the worst destroyers of inner life.

The coming of the machine and the very advantage we expected from it, the gaining of time, have resulted through its acceleration of exchange and transport in the spread of haste everywhere. And as soon as we take the smallest step into the business world, we are hunted and persecuted from morning till evening by hurry and fear of being late.

We should know that haste is one of the temptations of the big city and that, just as much as any other vice, it is a way of spoiling one's life and losing one's soul.

Let us not waste our time hurrying.

Remember that it is better to miss the train than lose your dignity.

Let us deliberately resist being swept away down this common incline. Let us purposely slow down our movements and steps, our speech and the course of our thoughts. Let us suspend our acts and above all our reactions, our outbursts of anger, our answers in conversation in order to recall awareness, even if only for a split second.

We shall take measures to avoid being caught unawares, and make our plans prudently when we have a busy day ahead, cutting out this or that task or engagement.

Even if we are the busiest people in the world, we can't avoid taking time off in order to sleep, eat, or wash. Let us keep a time every day, however much it costs us, for reflection, meditation, and prayer, for such care of ourselves is no less important than any other; indeed, it is much more so.

Nevertheless, some occasion always arises when charity, courtesy, or some other imperative duty tears us unreservedly away from our attempt to remain calm. It is in the heat of action that we must then find a remedy for haste by *inner suspension*.

Inner suspension is a form of self-recollection. It consists in repeating and understanding this: "My body is running because it must and I am even putting all my willpower into my legs; but I am not in the race, because I am not my body. I remain in my place watching my body run."

# MEDITATION

The purpose of meditation is the conversion of the intelligence, the senses, and the imagination; their reversal toward the inside so that they enter the inexplicable, invisible, essential living unity that is the true "I."

The true "I" is a point, a target one aims at, eyes closed.

"I" is a point, but that point is a hub. The slightest movement of the hub brings about an immense movement of the rim.

"I" is a point, but that point is a seed. There is more power in a seed, in which everything is gathered up into one, than in a spreading weathered tree. The whole of the oak was already in the acorn.

"I" is a point. That point is alive, one, and unique, as God is alive, one, and unique. A secret likeness, hidden in my depths, a likeness of which there is no image.

Nothing is narrower than a point. This point is the path to God, for I can only go to Him through what in me is like Him, and that is myself. It is the "narrow path" along which few venture. One and unique, every time, is the man who ventures onto it, whereas the great number take the broad road to outer darkness.

Meditation is generally sustained by a phrase, or an image, or a phrase applied to an image.

I must warn you right away against the presumption and self-indulgence of choosing your own theme of meditation and changing it whenever you like. That bad habit brings its own punishment, which is to see your themes, founded on no authority, topple and slide into each other. Now the theme is the house in which we should find shelter from bad weather, and it is not so dangerous to be in a storm as to be surrounded by crumbling walls.

So you must ask the person who initiated you to give you a theme, and you will tell him or her of your efforts, difficulties, discoveries, doubts and, God willing, your joy. You can tell your initiator alone, or talk to him in front of your fellow trainees so that your experiences and his advice may be of benefit to others.

Some spiritual masters give their disciples only one theme for the whole of their lives.

Whatever the case may be, a single theme should occupy us for several months, sometimes, several years. It is up to your guide to judge whether he should give you another if he finds you in difficulty or at a standstill.

To tell the truth, the theme only tints your meditation, for there is no other theme than I and God in my depths.

The image is only there to arrest your imagination, the phrase to arrest reasoning by rhythmical repetition. The image should not develop and give rise to others, nor the phrase explain; it should sink into you and become deeper by repetition.

The image or phrase should be consumed in meditation. The Hindus compare it to the fire board and the kindling stick that rubs as it turns in the hole in the center of the board. The board and the stick set fire to each other and the fire devours all.

I gave you the Tree of Life as a theme.*

The tree is a link between the earth and the sky, an aspiration of the whole earth. It is a living creature without knowledge of sin, pain, or filth, and a reminder of the First

* Shantidas was speaking to a group he had been working with some time. (Ed.)

Garden. It is a musical form creating itself from within, working in repose and expressing itself by its beauty. It is a great, inoffensive force in perpetual growth. The psalm says aptly that the righteous man will grow like a palm tree, or like a plane tree planted by a river.

Meditation on the tree is suitable for passing from the profane to the religious, from the bodily to the spiritual plane. It reconciles instead of opposing them, entails no risks, and hides nothing suspect.

But let it be understood from the outset that you are not to do these exercises out of curiosity or vanity or to show off, but because you aspire

> *to know yourself*
> *to love your neighbor*
> *to serve God*

because you understand that these three things are one and because you feel the need to acquire the strength, calm, and clarity required for them.

Having outlined the main exercises, let us come back to the technical details, remembering that goodwill and disorderly fervor are not enough.

The process is simple. It consists in silencing all inner argument, driving out daydreams, flooding yourself with such darkness as can receive the Light, pure and perfect darkness untroubled by false lights. Your night will see no star so long as it is blinded by electric bulbs. So turn out your lights if you want to contemplate. You have had a natural experience of contemplation in your deepest sleep. When an image arises in the midst of sleep, it takes on the force of reality. Likewise, when you have hushed all inner chatter, the tree will take shape all by itself. You will see it like the sailor who discovers, when the fortieth day of the voyage dawns, an island nearby on the curve of the sea.

Needless to say, the tree is not an end in itself, and there is no question of contemplating or worshipping a tree. But it is a means of piercing and purifying the darkness, which in its turn is a means of summoning the Light.

You may come up against incomprehensible difficulties. In that case, examine the state of your body. Is it empty and feverless, neither stimulated nor irritated, and well aired and calm? Face toward the north.

Is it a favorable hour? The best time is around dawn when everything in creation is rising and houses are quiet.

Is your posture right? Are you steadfast in uprightness?

Finally, and above all, are you perfectly relaxed? That is the most frequent and least noticed of stumbling blocks. In your eagerness to concentrate, you may be frowning and gritting your teeth and perhaps clenching your fists. In your early attempts, you will sometimes be attentive and tense, sometimes sleepy and absent-minded. You will probably have to alternate between states of tension and relaxation until such time as you can maintain the one within the other.

I suggested that you should absorb the image, fuse the image of the tree with the structure of your body so as to incorporate the image, build the tree trunk with the vertical line that runs through you and its great mass of foliage with your breathing.

You will fix all your attention on clinging to the image, not letting yourself be carried off by the wind or lifted up into the sky, and keeping your mind from wandering or flying away.

This exercise should enable you to become dense and deep, not sublime and airy.

And now, after arming you against the difficulties, I must put you on your guard against false and unexpected facility.

It may very well happen that from the start you feel uplifted, enlarged, infused with warmth, wrapped in light, visited by visions infinitely more beautiful than the tree, and beyond doubt beatific and divine.

Wait for what is to come and don't be so ready to believe yourself carried up into seventh heaven on the flying carpet of the Thousand and One Nights.

You are sitting motionless and breathing fully: in consequence, you are accumulating energy which is not flowing away in action. It is therefore being manifested in the mind. How does energy reveal itself in nature? By phenomena of movement, heat, and light.

What is taking place in you—heat, light, and rapture—is merely natural. You are enraptured, and rightly so, since it is good that something should happen. The phenomena and rapture are a good sign and nothing more.

As for the visions, they rise from the unconscious or depend on foreign influences which, even if spiritual, are not necessarily good. Don't let their strangeness exalt you. Drive them out bravely, just as you drive out your daydreams, although they are of another nature, and return to the Tree of Life where no serpent dwells.

"But," you will object, "how do you know that our visions (which we alone see) are not inspired from on high, and would it not be a great sin, if by chance they were, to brush them so bravely aside?"

My answer is that God bestows His grace on whom He chooses. You may indeed have been chosen. Remember, nevertheless, that mystic union is rare, as rare as miracles, or rarer, whereas the happy sensations we have been speaking of are not uncommon when one follows this method of preparation. In as great a measure as Faith and Hope are virtues and duties in everything that concerns God and salvation, doubt and humility are the rule for everything that concerns us personally. It is presumptuous to believe, without proof, that you are inspired. Prudence requires that if you believe you have had a revelation, you should first broach the subject with your spiritual guide, so that he may judge of its objective value. He also may be mistaken. What is least likely to be mistaken is the test of time and deeds. "A good tree can only give good fruit." If your virtues, your purity, your charity, your piety, your courage, and your wisdom shine forth, they will speak with authority of the holiness of the source from which they spring.

You may also make real progress without encountering any "phenomenon" and without perceiving that you are advancing, like a man digging out a tunnel. One day, with a stroke of the pickax just like all the others, he finds himself on the other side of the mountain, suddenly in the broad light of day.

Whatever the case may be, go on boldly. All other adventures may be doomed to failure. But not this one. The end of this one is gained beforehand: it is in you, it is yourself. It is therefore wise to dare.

> Blessed is the man . . .
> [Whose] delight is in the law of the Lord;
> And in His law doth he meditate day and night.
> And he shall be like a tree planted
> By the rivers of water,
> That bringeth forth his fruit in his season;
> His leaf also shall not wither;
> And whatsoever he doeth shall prosper.
>
> (Ps. 1:1–3)

*Depict in the spirit of your soul*
*The Tree planted in the Garden of the Heavenly Paradise.*
            —*St. Bonaventure*
                  (Traité Mystique de l'Arbre de Vie)

*The soul is a tree of life planted in the midst of the*
*living waters of the Life that is God. The principle*
*of our good deeds is this source at the center of the*
*soul where the tree of our souls is planted.*
                  —St. Theresa of Avila
                  (The Castle of the Soul)


# PRAYER

It is possible to distinguish five degrees of prayer:

(1) Prayer of Obligation
(2) Prayer of Rogation
(3) Lyrical Prayer
(4) Prayer of Contemplation
(5) Mental Orison

(1) *Prayer of Obligation.* Every religion teaches its faithful good manners, teaches them to say "Hail!", "Forgive me," and "Thank you."

It would be too much to expect that these words recited from memory, these expressions of exaltation, of rejoicing and lamentation, these celebrations at fixed times, should always be heartfelt. Besides, they are not intended to *express* what we feel but, on the contrary, to *impress* their meaning upon us by patient, docile, and persevering repetition.

The ceaseless recitation of their continuous, rhythmical

murmur, forever the same like the sound of the forest or the sea, is meant to mark us each time more deeply with its content and to mold and hammer us into its form.

But this happy result (happy because that form and its content are of immemorial origin and extreme beauty) is obtained only if the will to obtain it accompanies recitation.

Should the will be lacking, repetition miscarries: our attention, dazed by monotony and habit, is driven out by centrifugal force, and mechanical behavior sets in.

People laugh at the Tibetans with their prayer wheels that turn and sound in the wind. The gods are satisfied, they think, so they have paid their due. But Tibetans are not the only people to make wind grind out noise.

There are also the machines that go wrong and grate and come to a standstill; the Lord's Prayers rushed through and mutilated and mumbled, the skimpy signs of the Cross, the sketchy bows to the altar.

This is the time to remember the first of our ten rules: attention. And if we cannot always be fervent, let us at least be good-mannered and keep our minds in suspension, accessible and present. Prayer is first of all an offering up of oneself, but how can a present be presented by someone absent?

The second rule, too: uprightness, the natural direction of "elevation of the soul." Let us keep our uprightness whether we are standing or kneeling. Let us never pray in a stooping position, or curled up, or twisted, or humped, or lounging.

And the third, which is breathing, whether we are speaking or singing; let us pause and begin at the proper places, and make sure that the tone and the tempo are right.

Also remember the fourth: relaxation. Let us not fidget in our efforts to keep awake, nor screw ourselves up in our attempts at repentance, nor let our necks sag into our shoulders; and let us not hold ourselves stiffly either, nor frown in an effort to assume suitable gravity, nor let us wring our fingers in a gesture that means "See, Lord, how I cling to myself and my desires and fears!"

If we cannot attain fervor in our love of God, fervor which can only come from God, let us at least preserve the respect that depends on us, that extreme respect which the Bible calls the Awe of God. It will save us from mind-wandering, carelessness, and other unconscious blasphemy.

As for our duty to be worthy, this prayer compels us to recognize our own unworthiness in comparison with His Glory, yet glorifies us by that same comparison.

Prayer will teach us to submit our lives to the rule of rhythm. Yes, prayer, more than the practice of the fine arts, or a taste for them. And more than any other form of prayer, prayer of obligation. For then we shall be related, not to the rhythm of our own hearts, but to the rhythm imprinted by the Creator on the universe, translated by the Prophets into the Scriptures and translated into rite by tradition.

The detachment we shall ask for in our prayers is to succeed in "worshipping God in spirit and in truth" and in remaining faithful to our religion without any accompanying servility, sectarian or fanatical passion, and without rebelling.

Obligation is neither slavery nor constraint; it is a link offered, held out (*ob-*) to our free will. There is no honor, then, in revolting against it, and no more excuse for neglecting it than for forgetting a debt.

Linked to prayer of obligation is the ritual of public worship which is testimony, teaching, service, and sometimes communion and the celebration of feasts.*

---

* In the Ark, the day is sustained by five common prayers.

(2) *Prayer of Rogation.* Prayer in which we ask for what we want, a cry from our desires, our needs, our fears. Prayer that is much more free and in all likelihood more ardent than the other.

This kind of prayer is so natural that the popular meaning of the word *prayer* excludes all other and is synonymous with asking.

We may ask for glory, fortune, victory, and the downfall of our enemies, the recovery of health, happiness in love, or luck in the Irish Hospital Sweepstakes, but that is not prayer of obligation.

We are not even recommended to do so, merely permitted.

And perhaps only because of our weakness and ignorance, to relieve us of too heavy a burden, as an outlet or a consolation, or to throw some light on the muddy mixture of our motives.

Indeed, it is somewhat contradictory to turn prayer, that outstandingly religious act, into entreaty and twist it into personal or collective self-seeking, considering that the spirit of profit is naturally, unconsciously, and guilelessly irreligious, and that religion is gift and sacrifice, which are the contrary of profit.

This sort of prayer is always more or less tinged with sin. That is why Jesus gently pushes it aside and calms his disciples. "Wherefore take ye thought, O ye of little faith? For your heavenly Father knoweth that ye have need of all these things. He feedeth the fowls of the air and arrayeth the lilies of the field. Five sparrows are sold for a farthing. Are ye not much better than they? Seek ye first the Kingdom of God and his righteousness and all these things shall be added unto you."

Even the request for our daily bread in the Lord's Prayer is certainly due to a mistaken translation.*

At Mass, the Church makes us ask to be kept safe from all trouble, "ab omni perturbatione," and elsewhere implores, "Deliver us from War, Hunger, and Plague," which does not prevent these scourges from returning with the regularity of the tides upon the just as on the unjust, upon those who pray thus as upon those who do not pray, seeing that all alike continue to prepare these scourges and bring them about and inflict them upon one another and work for all their worth at deserving them.† Now, there is no point in throwing a stone up into the air and immediately praying, "O God Almighty, let that stone by miracle not fall on my silly head!"

The greatest good that can come to us from prayer of rogation is that we should discover our intentions spread out flat beneath the eye of God and that from His eye should come down the light we need to see and judge them.

Purification rather than satisfaction.

The acceptable request is the one we present like a cut flower: "If this is Thy Will, Lord, let it be done."

But (O ye of little faith) is it not better to say the simple words, "Thy Will be done"? For if His will is done, the Kingdom has come, and what more need we desire?

Deliver us, Lord, from every desire that is not desire of Thee. Come, and take Thy place in us.

(3) *Lyrical Prayer* seeks no other satisfaction than itself.

* *Epiousion* in the Greek text can never give *quotidianum* but obviously means "Give us now our more-than-substantial bread" or "Give us this day our bread-to-come" (*mahar* [Aramaic]—of tomorrow).

† Why and how this comes about is the theme of *The Four Scourges* (*Les Quatre Fléaux*).

Its happiness is to be the living link between the lover and the beloved.*

No rule can be laid down for it, since of itself it finds what to say according to "the law of liberty" (James 2:12), which is love.

> *Love, and do what you will.*
> —*St. Augustine*

Lyrical prayer, which is intimate in essence, can take collective forms such as public confession, inspired preaching, and prophecy.

(4) *Prayer of Contemplation* is free worship, but like prayer of obligation it has rules.

One prayer which is popular among Christians is the rosary, which deserves a place apart (perhaps the Stations of the Cross should come under the same heading, and among the Hesychasts, Greek and Russian alike, "the Prayer of Jesus").

The rosary consists of reciting prayers in series of ten while at the same time contemplating a "mystery." The mystery may be Joyful or Grievous or Glorious.

The fine point of the spirit being plunged into the mystery (that of the Nativity, for example, or the Crucifixion) and the mystery seen through the eyes of the Virgin, this breaks and interweaves the directions to be observed; it is obvious that thought cannot dwell on each word uttered, and that the recitation serves only as a background, like music without words, or the bare walls and shadowy spaces in a church, or smoke from incense.

---

* *The Book of the Lover and the Beloved*, by Raymond Lully (1235?–1315), is itself a lyrical prayer by which "understanding and devotion are increased."

Nevertheless, the recitation also prevents the theme of contemplation from unfurling and explaining itself or fraying into thoughts or images, and keeps it tightly enfolded under the veil.

(5) *Mental Orison* is silent prayer or, to put it more aptly, a suspension of prayer.

It is the exercise of "Presence to God and to Oneself" as taught by the great and ancient Carmelite tradition.*

I use the term *orison* and place it in the hierarchy of prayer out of respect for the holy masters of that school, for it is exactly what we call meditation. Like us, the Carmelites distrust (even if they do not refuse) "consolation through the senses, imagination and discursive reasoning, and the journey through *Nada, Nada!* Nothing! Nothing! that leads to 'Intellectual Vision.' "

Prayer and meditation do indeed meet at this supreme degree, which is ecstasy in truth.

Once more, this does not mean that we place meditation above prayer. For if we were to deal with meditation in detail, as we have done with prayer, we should have to distinguish five forms just as in prayer, or more precisely, four corresponding to the first four forms of prayer, and a fifth common to both:

(i) regular concentration;

(ii) staring fixedly at one point and condensing desire, or magic;

(iii) religious thought;

(iv) spiritual exercise;

(v) mystical meditation or mental orison.

* Read and above all meditate on the works of St. Theresa of Avila and St. John of the Cross.

(i) *Concentration.* This mental exercise is a rule with us. We do it in the early morning, just after the preparatory bodily postures and measured breathing. It is total immobilization of the outside and the inside. (This corresponds to prayer of obligation.)

(ii) *Staring fixedly and condensing desire.* These are the key to magic power. They are strictly excluded from our training as being suspect, dangerous if not diabolical, even when used for "white magic" and accompanied by extraordinary visions. (This corresponds to prayer of rogation.)

(iii) *Religious thought.* This is what people in the West usually mean when they use the word *meditation.* Interpretation of the Word of God, explanation of the Scriptures, reflection on the mysteries, dogma, sacraments, symbols, and rites, transmission of the teaching of the sages, lessons taken from the lives of saints and heroes, spiritual doctrine —whether given, received, or brought to maturity. Actually, that is exactly what we are doing now. (This corresponds to lyrical prayer.)

(iv) *Spiritual exercise.* The term is borrowed from St. Ignatius of Loyola, to whose famous treatise you should refer. In this exercise a subject is chosen, for example, a page from the New Testament, and one method consists in representing the scene to oneself, impregnating one's imagination and the five bodily and spiritual senses so strongly that one finally becomes an eyewitness and even one of the enactors of the scene. (This corresponds to prayer of contemplation.)

(v) We have already spoken briefly of the fifth.

Prayer is the simplest, most fundamental, and most complete of religious acts.

It is the sacrifice of the Word.

Now the Word was with God in the Beginning, and everything was created by it, and without it, nothing was created. In it every creature has its life (John 1:1–4).

Therefore, by offering up the Word, we offer up all things, and ourselves, and God Himself to God.

And now let us recite the common prayer of the Ark not as a prayer, but as a meditation of the third degree, I mean, weighing each word with the measure of what we have just said about prayer:

*O God of Truth*
*Whom various men name by various names*
*But who art One, Unique, and the Same;*
*Who art That-which-is,*
*Who art in all that is*
*And in the union of all who come together,*
*Who art in the heights and in the abyss,*
*In the heavens without end and the heart's secret shade*
*Like a tiny seed,*

*Praised be Thou, Lord, for our prayer fulfilled*
*Since this our prayer is its own fulfillment,*
*Since by addressing Thee together, Lord,*
*We elevate our will, purify our desire,*
*And are of one accord.*

*What more need we ask, if that is granted?*
*What more need we ask, unless that it should last, Eternal*
    *God,*

*All through our days and through our nights?*
*What more, unless to love Thee enough to love*
*All those who pray to Thee as we do*
*Enough to love those who pray and think in other ways*
*Enough to wish good to those who wish us evil*
*Enough to wish good to those who deny Thee or know Thee*
      *not,*
*The good of return to Thee.*

*Give us understanding of Thy law, Almighty God,*
*Fill us with marveling and merciful respect for every living*
      *thing,*
*Love with no reverse of hate,*
*The Strength and Joy of Peace,*

                                    *Amen.*

## DIG DEEP

*He is like a man which built an house and digged deep, and*
*laid the foundation on a rock. (Luke 6:48)*

Dig, dig deep into yourself. For your good and bad deeds
carry you outwards, your thoughts and education carry you
outwards, your opinions of other people carry you outwards.
All these are a forgetting and have no foundation. They can
and must be, but not until you have reached your inner
depths.

In Hebrew, a language rich above all others in poetry,
there are no abstract words, and the word *rock* means principle (a meaning handed down to the alchemists; the philosopher's stone is the principle of transmutation). Dig, and
you will find rock, the principle, the foundation. When

you have found rock, you can build your house upon it, and neither the flood of daily events nor the torrents of your own passions will prevail against it.

## JUDGE NOT

*Judge not.* Why does this precept come immediately after "Love thine enemies and be merciful"? And what exactly does judge mean?

Judging is breaking away and setting oneself above. One cannot judge things from below. Consequently, whoever judges sets himself up as superior to the person he is judging. His judgment implies his thorough knowledge of the law and his right to wield the thunderbolt of the avenger. It presupposes his perfect understanding of the person judged. When we judge our fellow man, who is in fact our equal, we are therefore putting him into a false position and unwittingly running a considerable risk.

## CHARITY

When asked by a Pharisee who is trying to catch him out, "What is the first commandment of the law?" Jesus answers, "Thou shalt love the Lord thy God with all thy heart, with all thy soul and with all thy mind, and thy neighbor as thyself" (Matt. 22, Mark 12, Luke 11). And the Pharisee, recognizing the authority of the text, can find nothing to say.

But what is this love which is not the union of marriage, the ardor of lovers, the harmony of friendship, or family closeness, but love of one's neighbor, that is to say, of just anybody, of whoever is there? This love which is neither a sweet and comforting outpouring of the heart nor reciprocal kindness, but a giving and a total giving up, without reticence or reckoning? To begin with, has it a name? Yes, and even a divinely beautiful name. It is called Charity. And if this name, which means "grace," has lost its savor, with what shall it be seasoned?* With what salt of fire?

Nowadays, people talk of "giving charity" and often it has no more to do with Charity than "making love" has with Love. No, Charity is not something one can hand out. It is uncreated, the very breath of God.

Charity is superabundance of justice and the law of freedom, a breaking of fetters and absolute deliverance. It is the reversal of self-love and covetousness. It is joy in suffering and spiritual sacrifice, the communication of grace, the gift and discovery of the essence, perfect knowledge and living truth, seven points I shall try to make clear.

First of all, it is important to understand that Charity is not an affection. If it were, it could not be the object of a commandment, for we can obey no matter how we are affected, but we cannot be affected in one way or another out of obedience. So the love that is required by "the greatest commandment" is not of the order of sensibility, but of will. It is not a sentiment but a virtue. This love does not touch just one aspect of our being, it sets the whole of us to work. *Thou shalt love with all thy heart, with all thy mind, with all thy soul and with all thy might.* After the heart, it gains the head; after the soul, it gains the body and is translated into act. This virtue is therefore the complement, the accomplishment, and the plenitude of our whole nature.

* The derivation of *caritas* or *charitas* from the Greek *charis* is questionable, I know.

Moreover, all love fills our measure and overflows. Everything I hate isolates me, hardens me within my limits, and restricts me, whereas I am increased by what I love. What are the limits of me and mine if not other people, their rights and strength? But if I love them, where are my limits? If I oppose my strength to theirs, their strength and mine annul each other. But if we join our strength, we double it. If I share other people's sorrows, their sorrow is lessened. If I share other people's joys, my joy is increased. I benefit from what I receive, more still from what I give.

That's all very well, but to quote Valéry,

> . . . *rendre la lumière*
> *Suppose d'ombre une morne moitié.**

If you are facing the sun, your back is in the shade and your whole body casts a shadow on the earth. It is the same with love. Every love that springs from the heart or the body has its counterpart of hate, and often the hate outweighs the love. If I love a woman passionately, I hate everybody who might do or wish her harm, as well as those who wrong me by not admiring her. In addition to which, I also hate whoever loves her too much and seeks to win her favors from me. And that is nothing. Should she by chance start loving somebody else and do me the supreme injury of finding happiness apart from me, my great love would drive me to deadly hatred of her.

And what words can describe the grasping, jealous attachment of families wallowing in their self-complacency and their quarrels? What can be said of their *affection*, except that the word resembles *infection* and is also used for

* " . . . to give back light
Supposes a dull half of shade."

*illness?* Theirs is the lukewarm staleness that sours the humors and rots the heart while the slime of indifference toward the whole world thickens. Wherefore Christ cried to the great crowds that followed him, "If any man come to me, and hate not his father, and mother, and wife, and children, and brethren, and sisters, yea, and his own life also, he cannot be my disciple," and asked, "Who is my mother? And who are my brethren?"

But what of the passion that sets thousands, millions of men on fire in the name of patriotic love or partisan fervor and uplifts them to such a pitch that for many it takes the place of religion?

Judge the tree by its fruit: war, sedition, massacre, captivity, oppression, and ruin. Such love is only a counter-hatred, and the proof is that, left to themselves, partisans and patriots alike will tear their fellow partisans and fellow patriots to pieces. The only thing that holds the horde together is common hatred of some other horde.

Yet, for all the degradation, damage, and crime it leads to, love is still the source of all life, and without it nothing is of any worth.

But how shall we recognize Charity if it is different from all other love? By this sign: it is a love without limits.

Now if the love that takes us beyond our own limits is itself limited, it takes us out of ourselves only to leave us in a blind alley. The limits of love are indifference, enmity, and reprobation. But in the eyes of Charity, no one is indifferent, no one an enemy, no one to be rejected, so where are its limits? Charity is infinite, infinitely good like God Himself, which proves that it belongs in God, indeed, is the very spirit of God. It goes out to each and all without consideration of persons, like justice, but how much better it is than justice. For justice is "a lesser evil," whereas Charity is the supreme good. Justice takes an eye for an eye, a tooth for a tooth, returns evil for evil so as to balance the scales of evil and prevent an excess of disorder. But Charity returns good for good and good for evil, and wherever malice opposes her, she redeems it with redoubled ardor, to break and burn the barrier.

It is therefore true to say that Charity is the superabundance of righteousness and the complement of the law. The words are not mine, but Christ's, since he says, "Except your righteousness shall exceed the righteousness of the scribes and Pharisees, ye shall in no case enter into the Kingdom of Heaven," and again, "If you love them which love you and do good to them which do good to you, what do ye more than others?"

*Quid faceretis amplius?*

Charity is what St. James calls the perfect law of liberty (1:25). Who is free if not whoever does what he wants to? But if I want to sin, exercising the free will given to me at birth, shall I be free, or shall I freely have chosen to enslave myself to sin, since it is written, "Whosoever committeth sin is the servant of sin" (John 8:34)? No, I am not free to sin. It is a liberty I *take*, which means I do not have it, and the would-be taker is taken.

If, on the other hand, I want to submit to the law, but do so reluctantly, am I free? Yes, since I am doing what I want to; no, since I am forcing myself.

Therefore I do not reach freedom through the law, nor in spite of it, for the law limits my free will and sin prevents my deliverance.

But if I love, is it the law that stops me from killing, stealing, deceiving, insulting the one I love? Is it the law that forces me to give him his due? I know nothing of the law and its restraint, but I neither violate nor abolish it. On the contrary, I accomplish it and fill its measure to overflowing. But I do not act at random (*Caritas non agit perperam,* 1 Cor. 13), nor do I rush into unseemly behavior. I obey the new law freely. Therefore St. Augustine says, "Love, and do what you will" ( *Ama et quod vis fac*).

Because of its infinite character, instead of imprisoning me, this love sets me free, for as long as love is limited, it is a tie, *attachment,* and therefore a hindrance to freedom.

Love that is irresistible and stronger than I can in no way deliver me or lead me to conquer myself. On the contrary, it will carry me away and sweep me to where I do not want to go. Its cause is outside me. I am chained by it to what I do not know, and it destines me to darkness.

If the strength of a great love is to make me grow, it must come out of my depths and my center. Therefore, the germination of charity is voluntary. It is a kind will rather than a kind sentiment. It is even a kind will which at first runs contrary to all my feelings, contrary to my unreasonable dislikes, my unjust preferences, my desires and my pleasures, my interests, and the objects of my admiration.

Charity is that conversion or reversal of all things which is announced and preached on every page of the Gospel. "Thou shalt burn what thou hast worshipped, thou shalt worship what thou hast burned" might be said to every convert. "Thou shalt hate what thou hast loved, thou shalt love what thou hast hated and them which hate thee, thine enemies. Thou shalt look upon thy brethren as strangers and the stranger as thy brother."

All human love is centered about two poles, self-love and covetousness. Self-love is the violent preference each of us feels for what he calls "me," the inextirpable root of all love. From this root grows a trunk named attachment by which self-love extends to our close relations, those we call "ours." The branches of the tree are covetousness or desire. Through it, our love goes out to others in return for enjoyment, profit, protection, or glorification.

Charity upsets this order. It is a love without ties or attraction. And whereas attachment keeps me within the circle of my family and people like myself, and attraction draws me toward brilliant, noble, generous, and refined persons, Charity pushes me toward the poor, the leper, and the convict, and makes me cross the sea to go to the help of a Chinese orphan, a black slave, or a savage.

But there is somebody even more difficult to love than the poor and outcast, and that person is my enemy, the enemy who attacks and makes a fool of me, for if I love him, I shall expose myself to ruin and ridicule, perhaps even to death. Yet the man who attains such love breaks his last fetter and approaches the perfection of the Heavenly Father, who "maketh his sun to rise on the evil and on the good, and sendeth rain on the just and on the unjust."

Such love goes against my nature and gives me no rest night or day. It spoils all my pleasures, for my pleasures disgust me in the midst of a suffering world. My privileges revolt me, my property becomes an intolerable abuse. I feel the hardship of others in my very flesh. Their misery lies down in my bed and harasses me.

So it is a difficult and dangerous love. It has as great a need of suffering for its fruition as other love has of happiness. It requires a stricter control of the senses than does any ascetic discipline. It is a purifying fire and a perpetual sacrifice. "I love charity more than sacrifice," says the Lord. For of all sacrifices, Charity is the truest and most worthy.

But this sacrifice leaves its victim alive and even renews life in him. And this is the sign that new life is born: at the height of the suffering and the fatigue imposed by service, joy fills you. Emptied of all spontaneous emotion, your heart is full to overflowing. Thus Charity is its own reward. But if you do good to others in order to do good to yourself, you are not charitable. Being charitable, that is to say, wanting someone else's good and forgetting yourself, is enough to unite you with those whose good you have achieved, even to your feeling their good as your own. But much more than the good, you feel the union you have created, and it is true to say that everything one has left is "given back an hundred-fold" in this very life.

Charity is therefore love transposed to the plane of the spirit, and it transports the lover to the Kingdom of Heaven.

I have often spoken of the passage from one plane to another as the reversal of the same laws. On the upper plane, we find the thing and its opposite making one and the same thing. We have seen that human love oscillates between two poles, which are self-love and covetousness. Now Charity is indeed the opposite of self-love since it is forgetting oneself for the good of others. It is the common love of which St. Bernard speaks, taking the word *common* not in the sense of vulgar but as indicating communion. Charity is also the contrary of covetousness or desire, which seeks enjoyment or advantage from others, Charity being a disinterested, chaste, and suffering love. But has the desire that in every man goes out toward what is stronger, more beautiful, and glorious than he so that he may find therein his good and his exaltation—has that desire been extinguished in the saint whom Charity forever drives toward the wretched? No, not extinguished, but consumed. The desire of the saint has gone straight toward the strongest, most beautiful, and most glorious of all, the Lord Himself, whom his soul, clad in righteousness and purity, has chosen as his spouse and for whom it sings the song of songs. Beside such joy, the rapture of lovers is only the game of children puddling in mud.

And has self-love been extinguished in him? No, consumed. Self-love is odious because it is an insufficient love of the self, just as covetousness is an insufficient desire for good and joy. Love of the self is enjoined in the greatest commandment and is the very foundation of Charity since it says, "Thou shalt love thy neighbor as thyself." If I did not love myself, how could I love him as myself? If I wanted my own downfall and destruction, how could I do good to him? It is not saints who want their own death and misfortune, but the vicious, the passionate, and insane. To love oneself, to want one's own good, is sane, wise, and saintly. But one must first know that one's good is salvation and bliss, and one must have self-knowledge.

Here is where the essential flaw in self-love appears: ignorance and misknowledge of the self. Indeed, what each of us calls "I," that which we cherish to the detriment of others in an attempt to triumph over the world, is what everybody sees and knows: a body, an image, and a name. But what a man could know of himself, by himself, in himself alone, that which is his being and his soul, remains foreign to him and uncared for. If he sought his own soul, he would come into conflict with no one. If he set off alone to find his own soul, he would join everybody else, since he would find the being common to all. That is how his self-love would become "common" love. Charity springs from a deep well, from what is deepest, most secret, and most inward in man: himself. But how can he give what he does not possess? What he does not know? What he has no hold on? "How can a poor man give to a poor man?" asks St. Catherine. "How can a dead man bury a dead man?" And elsewhere, "From self-knowledge springs ardent charity." We have to find the well from which Charity springs.

"Though I bestow all my goods to feed the poor, and though I give my body to be burned, and have not charity, it profiteth me nothing." Now, I can give all, and not have Charity. I can give my body as a woman in love gives her body to her lover, and give money as a prince gives money to a subject, in order to subject him further, but I cannot have Charity unless I have access to the source of Charity, which is knowledge of myself and of God.

How does the saint come to love the wretched with greater love than that of friends, or of man and wife? Does he not see that the person on whom he wastes so much love is not worth it? That he is old, ugly, ill, ungrateful, drunken, and guilty? The saint sees all that. He sees it only too well, but he does not believe what he sees, *he believes what he knows.* "In him there is what there is in me, what there is in God. This man is myself, this passer-by is God." Is it blasphemy to say, "This passer-by is God"? No, it is not blasphemy and the words are not mine, but the Lord's.

"Lord, when saw we thee an hungered, and fed thee? Or thirsty, and gave thee drink?" ask the disciples. "When saw we thee a stranger, and took thee in? Or naked, and clothed thee? Or when saw we thee sick or in prison, and came unto thee?"

"Inasmuch as ye have done it unto one of the least of these my brethren, ye have done it unto me" is the reply (Matt. 25:40).

By purification, then, by self-examination, by seeking the essence, Charity is attained, for being charitable is knowing, not with the tip of the intellect, but through trial of the whole being by fire, that the self in our being is the self in all.

Whoever is charitable can look at the most wretched and sinful of men and say, "That suffering, those sins are mine." He can look at the purest and greatest, Christ Himself, and say, "I should be He if I knew how to be myself."

Charity is the recognition of self in the other, concrete and living knowledge of being. Therefore it is entrance into the quick of truth.

## UNIVERSAL LOVE

A YOUNG MAN: Perhaps I'm a freak, but I'm not sure I like the love you describe as divine. I'm not sure I'd like to be loved with a love that consists in finding the same thing in everybody and in loving everybody in the same way.

SHANTIDAS: Your unwillingness arises from two misunderstandings concerning the *self* or the *same* and "everybody." These misunderstandings are due to my expressing myself badly and incompletely.

When I say that loving is finding the *same* or the *self* in other people, I don't mean that all souls are just as alike as two coins. The *self* can in no way be likened to a homogeneous space made up of points without any qualities of their own, these points being souls. *Self* does not mean uniform, nor does it mean identical. If that were so, then every time that by the grace of love I reached the depths of a being, I should be disappointed and impatiently exclaim, "The same thing over and over again!" But I call them the "same" because in each dwells the same marvel and the same mystery; because I find in them the same savor and worth as is myself; because I see them from the inside as I see myself from the inside; because they are unique as I am unique.

Charity is a blend of essences, a recognition, a knowing, but nothing could be less abstract or less general than such knowing. Charity directs itself in a purely personal and particular manner to living, concrete, and conscious human beings. It comes to the aid of their bodies and their needs. As for love of the whole of humanity, that is just so many words and serves to fill poems and political speeches. The Law of Religion has never said, "Thou shalt love everybody," but with wisdom and exactitude says, "Thou shalt love thy neighbor." In intention and quality, charity is infinite, but not in extent and quantity. It is spiritually and materially impossible for me to love multitudes of people I do not know, and to whom I can do no good. My duty is to love whoever is within my reach, to serve, know, comfort, and save him, to love in him the whole of humanity since he represents and contains it all.

## BLESSED ARE THE POOR IN SPIRIT

"Blessed are the poor in spirit," says Matthew, "for theirs is the Kingdom of Heaven." This is the first of the Beatitudes. The Latin text says *spiritu* and the Greek *pneumati*. In both cases, the meaning could be *poor in spirit, poor in the spirit, poor for the spirit, poor because of the spirit.* Luke says simply, "Blessed be ye poor." But the words were addressed to the disciples, of whom there can be no doubt that it was for the sake of the spirit that they had chosen poverty.

The poverty in question is therefore poverty such as it is commonly understood, that is to say, dire need. Blessed are the needy. But he is talking to the disciples. "Blessed are ye that hunger now," says Luke, "for ye shall be filled."

Luke therefore seems to indicate the meaning clearly:

poor in spirit, because of the spirit, they have deliberately dispossessed themselves because of the spirit in them, and have no need of the riches other men seek and cherish. The sense of "simple-minded" derives from the same principle. Stripping oneself of vulgar wealth is not enough. One must also strip oneself of that rare wealth which is acquired through the intellect and culture. A poor man, needy because of the spirit, may still be rich in satisfaction with his own learning. His cup may be brimming over with enjoyment of his own mind. But a man spiritually endowed must be able, or at least want, to renounce such riches and become simple with the simplicity that is the sign and symbol of unity.

For intellectual wealth has the same effect as other wealth: it procures easy and immediate artificial satisfaction. Wealth is bad because it procures immediate, easy, and artificial satisfaction: poverty is good because it gives a price to everything by making everything difficult and teaching whoever wants to overcome his own poverty—I mean *overcome*, not *flee*—by teaching him to free himself from desire and the object of desire. This is done by taking desire back inward and turning it toward an eternal object.

Now the effect of intellectual knowledge is to clutter up the soul with a multitude of objects. These divide it and multiply the soul's opportunities of being led astray. Why is wealth bad? Because it is an immense distraction, or at least, a temptation so strong as to be almost irresistible to be continually distracted. Distracted from what? From oneself. The temptation is no less, indeed, is even more secret and insidious when one's riches consist in idols, talent, knowledge, and riches of the mind.

So the idea evoked by the ordinary translation of "Blessed are the poor in spirit," the idea of naïve, stupid, uneducated people, should not be entirely rejected. Let us not forget the extreme rigor with which St. Francis, who had given himself up to poverty, excluded and rejected books, and how he cursed one of his disciples who had become a professor at the University of Bologna, cursed him with terrifying severity and without any hope of pardon. This gives us a sounding of how many meanings are bound up with each other in "poor in spirit."

The poverty meant, then, in the first precept of the Sermon on the Mount is total: poverty of the body, the heart, and the mind. Real and symbolic poverty. The needy are hungry and thirsty. They beg, hands outstretched. To hold out their hands, they place themselves on the lowest rung of the human ladder. They bow their heads, expose their own unworthiness, forget their pride, renounce the spirit of competition which teaches decent men to win a place in the sun at all costs. The attitude of the disciple who wants to enter the Kingdom of Heaven is like that of the needy. He takes the lowest place and holds out his hand. Be needy in spirit, be beggars for the spirit, beg for the bread of the spirit from whoever can give it and do not be afraid to humble yourself before him as the beggar does to any passer-by. That is the condition, and when that is achieved, the spirit itself is achieved, for Jesus did not say, "theirs will be the Kingdom of Heaven," but, "theirs is the Kingdom of Heaven." By the mere fact of stripping yourself bare, you enter the Kingdom of Heaven completely, here and now.

If you are not in the Kingdom of Heaven, there is some flaw in your renunciation. You are somehow attached to somebody or something. There is some treasure in your inner depths which you have not given up. If you had given it up absolutely, victory would not be a promise. You would know it yourself for a fact.

# THE PURE IN HEART,
# THE PEACEMAKERS,
# AND THE PERSECUTED

The heart is like the water of a lake. When it is troubled and stirred, you no longer see the water. You see only waves and broken and twisted reflections of things. But when the water is calm and pure, you can see its transparent substance and the living creatures who live and swim in it. You can see into its very depths, and deeper than its depths, you can see the image of the sky.

*Blessed are the peacemakers: for they shall be called the children of God.*

A peacemaker does not mean a peaceful person. Peacemakers are not people who stay still or avoid getting hurt. Christ himself said, "I came not to send peace but a sword," and, "I am come to send fire on the earth."

Peacemakers *make* peace. They make it out of nothing, make it out of disorder, create it as God created the world from nothing, molded it in the mass from chaos. And when God had created the world, *He saw that his work was good,* that is to say, that peace reigned there, which is the mark of God. *Peace* has the same root as *pact,* the same root as *compact.* Whatever is harmoniously united in justice is at peace. Peace is fulfillment in unity. What breaks peace is the sin of separation, pride, curiosity, ambition, and greed. A peacemaker is someone who rids himself and all around him of pride, curiosity, ambition, greed, and also of laziness and fear, someone who "sows love where there is hate, forgiveness where there is offense, union where there is discord," according to the prayer we say daily. A peacemaker is someone who works untiringly to restore God's work on earth. He can therefore be called by the highest title that can be given to a creature, the title that befits Christ Himself, the title of Son of God, since by his work he continues the Creator's and makes himself in the likeness of God.

*Blessed are they which are persecuted for righteousness' sake: for theirs is the Kingdom of Heaven.*

The eighth Beatitude ends like the first: *for theirs is the Kingdom of Heaven.* It is not enough to have detached oneself, to have accepted or sought for poverty, sorrow, and suffering, to have accepted it with hope of consolation, to have purified oneself so as to understand the utter purity of Heaven; the charitable, the truthful, the hungry and thirsty for righteousness, the peacemakers who have found the peace the world cannot give must still suffer other men's injustice, and suffer it bodily. For then they will be able to rejoice, since this injustice can do them no harm or destroy anything in them other than what must be destroyed, what they themselves want to destroy. Therefore their persecutors are merely acting with God's permission and their own consent, and although they act in the belief that they are harming them, they are indeed delivering them from useless goods, among them the very breath of life, for it is written, "He that loseth his life shall find it."

## HUMILITY

A great servant of God and speaker of truth* excluded humility from the vows he and his followers took because,

---

* Mahatma Gandhi.

he said, "one cannot want to be humble." One can only force oneself to speak with modesty, which is clever, and so one lapses into hypocrisy.

Indeed, one cannot become humble through trying. On the other hand, one cannot not become humble if one's attention is constantly turned toward the grandeur of God. For immensity is a measure nothing can stand up to. To become aware of God's infinite greatness is to become aware of the nothingness of all things including oneself. To consider oneself worthy of consideration and to behave with self-assurance and self-importance is simply to forget God. To affirm God is to reduce oneself to nothing. There can therefore be no religion (which is an affirmation of God and a link between God and man) without humility.

A method frequently recommended for learning humility is remembering one's faults, one's past mistakes, things one is ashamed of. That is a good thing to do, but it does not always lead to humility, for the proud are constantly stumbling on such thoughts and it only irritates their pride. Likewise, if you want to cure someone else of pride, even a child, it will always be wrong to humiliate him. If you do, you will lay up explosive stores of hatred in him and terrible revenge. One thing only can cure a man of conceit, and that is confrontation with celestial things.

## CREATION

Therein lies the great mystery of the grandeur of God, which, unlike space, is not a vast, lifeless, unmoving void, but a living and ever-increasing immensity. This perpetual increase is creation. Thus the infinite increases in the finite, and greatness overflows into smallness.

Now God's abundance overflowing into the creature, His immensity enclosed in a particular point, is the soul, and the purpose and destiny of the soul are increase of the divine infinity hidden within her substance like a tiny seed. Therefore the soul can say—*must* say—"I, the infinitely small, magnify the Infinitely Great."

## HOW TO SING

Shall I give you some advice on how to sing? Only one thing matters. Keep it constantly in mind and you will find that the rules of good music will proceed from it logically. It is this: Recall yourselves.

*What?* you ask. *What must we recall?* I said, *Recall yourselves.* I didn't tell you to recall something. Recall nothing but yourselves. Recall into yourself the you that always wants to go and fritter itself away outside. Bring it back into its place, collect yourself.

Next to prayer and meditation, singing is the happiest of returns to the obvious, to the source, to the garden of childhood. It is Paradise Regained. At its origin, it is a powerful invocation of the essential, a search for purity, pacification, and inner union, a search for the Presence.

So do not sing for amusement. That would be upsetting the order of things, and your own downfall. Do not sing when you are absentminded. That would be blasphemy. Do not sing between your teeth, and never whistle. That would be defilement, a lack of self-control under the eyes of God, an indecency like dirtying one's pants.

Don't let your attention be distracted when you sing. In the first place, don't let your own singing distract your attention and carry you away. Don't wallow in your song with drunken sobs if it is languorous, or burst into laughter if it is lively. Let your voice go out freely, but do not go out of yourself with it. Don't let your own voice, its strength or soaring lightness, distract you. Vanity is a flaw which immediately betrays its presence by noisy and obtrusive buzzing.

Don't be distracted by listeners, and don't worry about the effect your singing may have on them. Sing as if you were alone. Each of them will hear your voice rising as though from his own depths, and that is where harmony has its only source.

Don't let your attention be distracted for a single moment from the true pitch of each note, which is the probity of the singer and too rare a virtue. Remember that whenever your attention wavers, your voice loses pitch.

Don't let your attention be distracted from what you are saying in your song. The rhythm, the movement, the right tone of voice will follow of themselves. Rhythm is a knee pushing up the dancer's skirt from inside and making folds in the cloth, not a hammer breaking up a stone by beating on it from outside.

Beating time and bars should be used for sightreading, but all that scaffolding should be done away with when the front of the house is built, and the meaning of the phrase should shape its rhythm.

Don't let your attention be distracted from the tune when it rises and falls, curves and returns to its starting point. That is the sign of the return of the seasons and of your own return to yourself.

Let the purity of your voice be a measure of the purity of your soul. Let your voices in tune pledge the harmony of your hearts.

And now, go and sing! May God watch over you as you travel along the highroads of France.

## FASTING

Fasting is an exercise that consists above all in not thinking about your fast, just as chastity consists in not thinking of women. It tears the spirit away from the belly. It makes you strong by proving to you the strength of the spirit. It makes you humble by reminding you, through suffering, of your limits.

Avoid letting your thoughts wander to steaming dishes and loaded tables if you don't want to lose all the fruits of your fast.

Remember the hungry people of this world and pity them with a heart grown more tender.

Whoever fasts becomes transparent.

Others become transparent to him.

Their suffering enters him and he is defenseless against it.

So take care to stop up your senses by eating well if you don't want to be devoured by charity.

## KEEP QUIET

Be silent much in order to have something to say worth hearing. But again be silent to hear yourself.

Silence is the rind of the fruit, without which everything dries up before autumn.

If you speak of your love, you love with your lips only.

If you speak of your sacrifices, the approval of your listeners seems less vain to you than deliverance and wisdom.

If you speak of your visions, others will not see them, and you will soon cease to see them yourself.

If you speak of your occult powers, your boasting will drive them out of you like an exorcism.

If you speak of the most precious thing you have, the only thing that belongs to you, of the good you have done, it is sold: you have had your reward in words.

## COLD

Do not protect yourself from cold by wrapping yourself in a woolen cocoon.

You are not afraid of exposing your face to mountain snow and the sharpest winds, yet your face is the most delicate surface of your skin.

So, step by step, go as far as possible toward nakedness, which alone is sound and holy, so that your whole body becomes your countenance.

Rid yourself each morning of the clamminess of sleep by bathing in cold water. Even if you must break ice to find it.

Cover yourself only to meditate, read, write, or sleep. Remain uncovered so long as you are moving. If cold stings you, quicken your movements. Do not fear the wind on sweat. Let your life not depend on a draft and a rag.

## SICKNESS

If you fall ill, treat the illness by showers and sweating: give it a jolt lest, being at ease, it stay with you.

But if fever gets the better of you and your legs give way, look for a dry corner and lie down out of the way.

Fast, drink water, and wait. Help your illness to pass by not thinking of it.

There is only one cure for all diseases: patience.

If your time has come, die with good grace.

Nothing is more vain than to want to put off the hour that will come all the same.

And nothing is more vulgar than to insist.

## KEEP STILL

Such is our need to flee our own presence that the most convenient attitude becomes torture after two minutes.

Your limbs rolled up and knotted, establish yourself in an unshakable position.

There, do nothing other than doing nothing.

Do it perfectly.

Don't turn your head, don't bend it, don't let your backbone sag, don't flicker your eyelids, don't cough, don't brush off the ant that is climbing up your wrist nor heed the pins and needles tingling in the foot your thigh is weighing on.

Possess your limbs, do something with them.

Become like a thinking log.

If birds start pecking round your knees, angels are hovering near.


# TIME AND LIFE

Don't waste your time earning your living.

Earn your time: save your life.


# CONTROL OF THE BODY

Since your body cannot follow you into steadfastness, keep it constantly on the move so as to put its anxiety off the track.

All day long, keep it walking or working; stop it only for sleep. If for one single moment you cease to busy your body, it will busy you.


# WATCHFULNESS: THE FOOLISH VIRGINS

Only one thing is missing. But when this thing is missing, all the rest falls short, and it is just as if they had never had anything, as if they had never been virgin, or beautiful, or called. They have not watched. They should have watched, they should have prepared, and they have not prepared. Even to fall asleep, they should have prepared, for wise and foolish virgins alike slumbered and slept while waiting for the coming of the bridegroom. Even to fall asleep, they should have been watchful. Lack of watchfulness is the eighth capital sin: distraction. A capital sin in the true sense of the word, the head sin, head and root of all others. The eighth deadly sin, or, if you like, the first, since all the others reduce to it. What else are anger, pride, gluttony, lust, sloth, and all the others but distraction, lack of heed to the essential?

Heedlessness entails all the rest. Heed to anything whatever saves everything and saves from everything. It is the only saving grace, the only way out from anxiety, disorder, and perdition. The man who is heedless and careless has everything to fear. Whoever has no fear because he is too heedless to understand the danger he is in, has everything to fear. Whoever offers the excuse that he has *forgotten*, stands accused and condemned by his own excuse.

You all know the disastrous practical consequences of heedlessness. You know that through heedlessness you can die or kill more readily than out of evil passion or diabolical cunning, but you are not in the habit of considering this practical failing as a lack of goodness, a clearly determined fault which calls for repentance as much as, if not more than, any other fault. Indeed, heed is worthless and cannot be a safeguard unless it is heed of the essential, whereas the most common and least worthy heed is heed of everything that does not save, everything useless, or everything that serves our desires. In reality, it is not heed at all but, on the contrary, letting oneself be carried away and drawn out of oneself, absorbed by desire. It is not the heed that can be called watchfulness. The heed that saves is one and the same thing as conscience. It is heed of the self, fear of self-loss and self-dispersion, a conscious and constant effort of self-recollection, and the fruit of that effort is admirably represented in this parable by the oil in the lamps. There is no use whatever in having a lamp if one has nothing to put in it. Generous impulses are of no use if there is no substance behind them. They are merely illusions of generosity, another form of self-dispersion, one more way of abandoning oneself to natural inclination; and although the inclination may be good or judged good by others because they find it pleasant or useful, it is not good in itself and is worth nothing because it costs nothing. You must take heed to have oil in your lamp as well as to have a lamp and light it. Keeping the oil for yourself, or spilling it on yourself and staining your clothes instead of feeding the flame with it, amounts to having no oil, for one must have the oil, the lamp, and the match, all three at once, and not just one of the three.

The virgins go to the wedding and they must take heed to light their lamps so as to be present at the moment of union and united with those who are becoming one. That is what each must pay heed to. It is written that many are called but few are chosen, which seems unjust, and would be unjust if we did not know what the words mean. For the key is here: not only many are called. All are called. The call is to all living creatures. But of what avail is it to the deaf and the sleeping? All the angels in Heaven may call, God Himself may call, and cry out, shedding blood and tears, and threaten, but what can God Almighty do with such nothingness? What can He do for the distracted, the absent, those who pay heed to everything except His call?

To be ready for the call is to be awake. No one but yourself can awaken you spiritually, and it is the first of your duties. Wake up! Let us wake up, for we are asleep, sleeping a dreamless sleep, the dreamless sleep of ignorance or imbecility, or the sleep full of the dreams that are our own merits and virtues. How can the sleeper awake? How can we light in ourselves a spark of watchfulness and conscience? By taking heed, by heeding little things that would be useless and insignificant if they did not develop our attention. Cultivate attention to little things, accompanied by detachment from all things. For attention accompanied by attachment is useless, and is not attention, but absorption.

Attention to things should be practiced, not for desire or the acquisition of things, but for the acquisition of attention. Things should be a means, and desire of things an occasion, to exercise vigilance and detachment. Vigilance and detachment give conscience, and conscience constantly awakened, or rather, more and more constantly awakened, gives you the store which is the oil in the lamp.

See how, in this parable, possession of this oil is placed even higher than charity, since the foolish virgins ask the wise to give them some and the latter rightly answer, *We cannot, for we should not have enough ourselves. Go and buy some.*

We cannot, because it would be imprudent and foolish. Save others by saving yourself. Do not think you can save others by losing yourself. Save yourself to save others, as wisdom demands, as wise and complete charity requires. Whoever cannot swim does not have to jump into the water to save a drowning man, for both will drown, or else it will take twice the trouble to haul them out. It is charitable, necessary, and generous to jump into the water only when one knows how to swim and has some chance of pulling the other man out. One cannot teach others when one knows nothing oneself. One cannot advise others when one does not know how to give oneself. One cannot give what one does not have. The first duty is to have.

To have, where the spirit is concerned, is not a result of

fortune or chance. All who have, in this domain, have acquired and kept, have known how to keep, and that is why they have the right to give. Those who want to give, but have not, are generally not moved by charity but by pretension, because giving implies having. The fool who makes the gesture of giving without having gives himself the illusion of having and the pleasure of shining in the eyes of other men and perhaps in his own.

## THE REWARDS OF WORK

How can one disentangle oneself from riches, yet live? There are only two possible ways. Either accept being a beggar, take to the road, and preach, with no money and only one tunic, as Christ recommends to his disciples, and as itinerant monks do today. Or, as we\* do here, take the middle path and seek, through work, not to acquire riches but to keep poverty, gain freedom, and show the way of liberation to others, without any desire for outward prosperity or the security that does such harm to the rich.

Their security is as false as their freedom and as their generosity, for indeed, no creature lives in greater fear than a rich man. He is perpetually afraid, afraid of thieves, afraid of being taken advantage of, afraid of revolution, afraid of losing his wealth. We must accept wholeheartedly that goods do not belong to us and that danger is good, that the danger of finding ourselves disarmed and destitute is good, and that whoever has laid up his treasure in Heaven does not fear the loss of all his other goods. For whoever has left his father and his mother, his son, his brother, his sister, his

\* The Companions of the Ark.

house, his wealth, and his slaves, and has ceased to be slave of his wealth, his goods, his father and mother and brothers and sisters and sons and daughters will receive all riches a hundredfold, and heavenly and spiritual treasure too, in this very world.

Yes, in this very world, for what is the rich man seeking? He is seeking to excel, and thinks he will find excellence in an abundance of goods. He wants to live more fully and more broadly and seeks thousands of opportunities to become greater or make manifest a conventional and illusory greatness, and the accumulation of goods makes him feel a kind of searing pride instead of that impression of inner growth which alone gives joy. In search of a thousand vain pleasures, and the unique, furious pleasure of the conqueror, he pays with money for his magnificence and his joy, and the great evil the rich man suffers is the temptation of distraction, just as his great business is entertainment and making a show, which disperses and destroys the inner substance. That is what worldly wealth and power are: artificial deviations from spiritual grandeur and inner joy of which they are a caricature, a hideous caricature with a counterpart of wretchedness, since the riches of this world are limited and badly distributed by design. If some have too much of a thing, others inevitably have less, and those who have much easily acquire more, whereas those who have too little have almost mortal difficulty not to lose all.

What the wealthy of this world seek outside, the poor in spirit find a hundredfold within. What the former acquire apparently and conventionally, the latter acquire inwardly, in reality and in truth. That is how they store up treasure thieves cannot steal and rust cannot corrupt.

And now let us go on to the strange parable of the workers in the vineyard. This is not a jump but a natural transition since we have just been speaking of reward and treasure in Heaven, and Jesus has promised His disciples twelve thrones almost equal to His own.

The workers have been summoned for their pay, and we already know what the pay in question is. It is obviously Grace and Salvation. And the latecomers, those of the eleventh hour, who had been called at six or seven in the evening, receive (to their astonishment, for they had asked for nothing) a day's hire. They are given the coin of Grace and Salvation; and those who bore the heat of the day expect to receive more, but are also given Grace and Salvation, the same coin.

What sort of justice is this? Divine justice, concerning which we are never spared the knowledge that it differs from human justice. But that does not mean that it is injustice. It simply means that divine reckoning differs from human reckoning and is not so stupid, for human intelligence and the spirit of complaint cannot understand Grace and Salvation, just as human intelligence cannot understand whatever is infinite.

Grace and Salvation are infinite things, and what can two or three infinites equal? They are equal to *one* infinite. There can be no proportion between heavenly reward and the human action that merits it, for no action ever merits it. Earthly action deserves earthly reward. Action well done deserves success, no more. But action which is work in the vineyard of the Lord is rewarded by something entirely different and disproportionate to its worth. The Master of the House, God Himself, hires the laborers and pays them according to what is right. In the same way He called the Prophets and kept His covenant with His chosen people and would still keep it if His chosen people remembered their being chosen.

God is just: at the very least, just. He is also much more than just. He is kind. He is "rich with the riches of iniquity," as is said in the parable of the unjust steward, riches of indulgence.

Why are the latecomers to the Lord's work late? They answer for themselves, "Because nobody hired us." Although they have not borne the burden and the heat of the day, they did at least wait in readiness throughout the day, waiting to be called, and that is what is asked of every man: to be available, to be ready to answer the call, to refuse every false summons, to stand waiting. No sooner did the Master of the Vineyard come to hire them than they went, asking nothing, aware that they would be given what was right, and more still.

What is required of the Lord's laborer is an inner disposition toward giving and work. Work without this inner disposition is worthless. But work with this inner disposition serves everything, fills the measure at the start, overflows every measure. There is no point in wondering whether somebody who has renounced everything had great wealth to renounce. If a man has renounced only ambitious dreams and wretchedness, he will receive as much for his renunciation as the renouncer of a throne and palaces. And whoever devotes himself as fully, strongly, and courageously as he can to prayer and exercise, without thought of reward, will also be fulfilled.

"Who then can be saved?" the disciples ask, anxious and "extremely amazed." And Jesus answers, "With men this is impossible but with God all things are possible." And this answer takes us back to the first, the one He gave the young man. *Why dost thou call me good? There is only one that is good: God.* The work of salvation is not a human work, a natural work, a work that can be outwardly measured, measured by greatness of effort or tenacity of effort or by the cost of renunciation. It can only be measured by an inner measure that belongs to God alone. Salvation does not depend on any outer circumstance, nor on our courage in surmounting events. It depends on our independence of outer things, on giving up our own will so that God's work may be done in us.

## THE LORD'S PRAYER

"When ye pray," says Jesus (Matt. 6:7–8), "use not vain repetitions, as the heathen do: for they think they shall be heard for their much speaking. Be not ye therefore like unto them: for your Father knoweth what things ye have need of, before ye ask him."

If He knows beforehand, what point is there in asking, even in few words? For God, who sees in secret and hears in silence, there is no point. For us, there is. We need words for our thoughts to become comprehensible, for our feelings to become consistent, for our impulses to find direction. Prayer is its own fulfillment, since the first of God's mercies is to address us to Himself, attach us to Him, and let us communicate with Him inwardly. By virtue of words, desire rises to consciousness; by virtue of consciousness it is enlightened, vivified, and strengthened, exposed to the light of divine truth. Clearly, nothing obscure or impure can subsist there. At that moment, desire is offered up, that is to say, reversed. Indeed, the nature of desire is readiness to take, whereas here, by virtue of prayer, it opens and gives itself up like a flower, even like a cut flower. Thus our asking leads us to detachment from what we are asking for. It suffices that prayer, springing from desire, leads us into the presence of God, the supreme good, for the particular good we wanted to seem null and vain. That is why in perfect prayer, wanting is reduced to little or nothing. Such is the Lord's Prayer, taught us by the very God we pray to.

*Our Father which art in Heaven.* The first word worthy of our attention is the first one. *Our.* Not *I* am praying: *we* are. Whether we pray together or alone, it is always *we*. We are praying to the God and Father of all men. There is a remark in the Gospel, "Where two or three are gathered together in my name, there am I in the midst of them." Why? Because the unity of God is not abstract, nor is it singular. His unity is in itself relation. Not simply unity, but union. Where two or three are gathered together in My name.

Two or three terms are set and the relation establishes itself. The relation is the name in whose name these two or three are related. When we say *Our Father which art in Heaven,* the first word disposes us to gather into ourselves the whole of humanity and pray in the name of all our brothers, present or absent, living or dead.

*Our Father.* Jesus brings about a great mystic revolution in the tradition of Israel when He teaches his followers to give to God, the Almighty, the Most High, the Lord of Hosts, the name of Father. This revolution is a return to origin.

Indeed, primitive peoples all worship the souls of their fathers mingled with the forces of nature, then risen to Heaven whence they still watch over the tribe. This may well be the origin of the heathen gods, since the foremost among them is named Jupiter, that is to say, Jov Pater, or God the Father.

But it is one thing mistakenly to divinize the souls of our ancestors and another to call the true God "our Father," the god who is *That Which Is*, whose name is *I am*, the God who is clad in the terror of lightning, the God whose glory Moses could only behold with his back turned, since no man can look it in the face without dying. Jesus broke down the ramparts of terror and estrangement into which this awe and humility had grown. He taught that love bridges distance and crosses chasms, and that the invisible and vertiginously high King of Heaven is present and perceptible in the secret of the heart.

*Which art in Heaven.* Why is Heaven the place of divinity? Is it not true that God is everywhere? It is true, but the sky makes His presence manifest, being open, immense, circular, high, and pure. Mountains rise into the sky, and mountains represent the principle, the rock of stability. Stars shine in the sky or firmament, and the word *firmament* means *that which is firm and does not change*. Although clouds shrink and ruffle and veil it, we know that the sky behind them remains unchangingly bright. From the sky comes light, and light is the primordial reality, the material reality that resists all the laws of matter and reigns over all things. Shining equally on all things, eternally vibrant and beneficial, a joy to the eye and the heart, it is truly the first image, the imageless dazzling image of Divinity.

*Our Father which art in Heaven, hallowed be Thy name.* Why is His name insisted on? Why is it so important that the name of God should be respected and hallowed, holy on our lips as in reality? Because this name has its foundation in reality. It is not an abstraction, not a convention. The name is of primordial importance in religion. It is of primordial importance that it should be spoken exactly, or, if not spoken, thought exactly, because, without it no condensation, no concentration, and no accord are possible between people praying together. Do you see how the words *Thy name* remind us here of the first word *Our?* Without the name to relate us, there is no "We" and no link. You know that we are multiple, not only in numbers, but within ourselves. We are a vague and contradictory multitude, brutal and stupid if we have not laws, rules, signs, and names to guide us and gather us together, each within himself and one with another. It is by its power to concentrate, and not only by its meaning, that a word has power. In this power of concentration lies the secret of magic. What gives a magician power for good or evil is his power to condense and master thought and force it in a certain direction. Experience has proved that thought condensed, willpower concentrated and projected, without action, toward its target, has efficacity over things. Therein is the principle common to magic and religion. How, and with what intention, the principle is applied is what distinguishes the magician from the worshipper and the priest. A man who prays can and should be a great "white" magician, innocent of the will to be powerful, but powerful by his goodwill. And if he is not powerful, he is not good, for goodwill without willpower is worthless, and absentminded prayer is a lie told to oneself that fools nobody.

*Hallowed be Thy name.* Why is blasphemy a crime, when we know perfectly well that the blasphemer is not thinking of what he is saying? That is the crime, the whole crime. We have no right to utter such a name without thinking of what we are saying. *Thou shalt not take the name of the Lord thy God in vain* is as strong and absolute a command-ment as *Thou shalt not kill.* For it is almost better to kill a man who will die anyhow than to kill His name by speaking it without thinking. The eternal name, the name by which men live, the name that makes everything be, the name that gives worth to all the rest, the name that rouses the will, co-ordinates our powers, justifies law, and illuminates all truth.

*Hallowed be Thy name. Thy Kingdom come.* Thy King-dom. The Kingdom of God has been promised for the end of time. Why must we ask for it? God makes the Kingdom of Heaven, not we. But have you noticed that from the be-ginning of this prayer, we have asked for nothing for our-selves? We have asked for nothing, we have disposed our desire toward acceptance.

*Thy Kingdom come.* It will come, but what matters is that we should desire it, so that it does not come to our confusion. It rains on the just and the unjust, and mis-fortune befalls the wise man and the fool. *What hath the wise more than the fool?* asks Ecclesiastes. *The wise man's eyes are in his head; but the fool walketh in darkness; and I myself perceived that one event happeneth to them all.* The same things happen to all of us, good and bad. The Kingdom of God has been there since the beginning and is open to all, but few enter. In spiritual life, as we were saying, the first thing that matters is our attitude, the attitude of acceptance, sincerity, and courage. Whatever happens is in itself neither here nor there. I mean that everything, good or bad, can turn to good when the attitude is good, and to bad when the attitude is bad. Even the coming of the Kingdom of God is a misfortune for those who refuse to enter.

*Thy Kingdom come, Thy Will be done on earth as it is in Heaven.* His will is done in Heaven, but on earth, the daughter of Heaven, His will has not yet been done. To see this is a great mystery. The will of the Almighty has not been done on earth, so where is His Almightiness? Is it limited, then, by wretchedness and mischief, by evil and death? We must conclude that His Almightiness is not what we imagine it to be, but greatly surpasses our imagination since it has the power to curb itself at will. We must conclude that God who can do anything does not want to be able to do anything and refuses to exercise all His power. Why? So that we and all spiritual beings (and perhaps all beings are spiritual to a certain degree) may, according to their degree, exercise divine power. That is the gift of life, the gift of freedom which means that we are not pushed about in life like billiard balls on a table, or dropped into it like stones into the void. Something depends on us, even if our destiny is traced beforehand and our happiness and misfortune and various adventures and accidents have been allotted us from the beginning. There is something which is not given, and that is: *how we accept our lot*. It is the degree of conscience we shall acquire and our freedom, the freedom that depends on conscience. People ask if man is determined or if he has free will. He has, but he is determined according to the extent that he ignores that he has it. Effective freedom is not given but has to be acquired. That is why we have to be aware that we are also responsible for our ignorance, our forgetfulness, and for what serves as an excuse to most people: that they cannot do otherwise than they do.

*Thy Will be done on earth as it is in Heaven*. With this sentence, the first part of the prayer ends, the part which is acceptance and glorification, and the second part, which is request, begins. The request is a sober one: *Give us this day our daily bread* (Luke 11). It almost means, "Give us no more than bread, give us what we need to subsist, do not give us the surplus that is going to carry us away and destroy us." It is written that man does not live by bread alone. And in fact, Matthew in his version says "our supersubstantial bread" (Matt. 7). Give us our natural bread and give us our supersubstantial bread which is Thyself.

*And forgive us our debts as we forgive our debtors*, according to Matthew. And according to Luke, *And forgive our sins for we also forgive everyone that is indebted to us*. The French translation we usually recite (*Remets-nous nos dettes*) has no doubt the correct meaning but it is a paraphrase, not a translation. And it is audacious indeed to have changed the words that the Lord Himself put into our mouths. Not in vain does Christ speak of sin as a debt and recall the rate at which it will be reckoned. We shall be measured with the measure we use to measure others. Give and it will be given unto you, judge not that thou be not judged, absolve and you will be absolved. But how can I speak in this way, as if I had forgiven other people's wrongs toward me from the bottom of my heart? Can I pray and lie at the same time? It would be better to abstain from prayer until I have prepared myself properly, for I have been warned (Matt. 5:23–24): . . . *if thou bring thy gift to the altar, and there rememberest that thy brother hath ought against thee; Leave there thy gift before the altar, and go thy way; first be reconciled to thy brother, and then come and offer thy gift.* The request is two-edged. We ask God for forgiveness and at the same time demand it of ourselves. Thus prayer develops and sometimes creates the inner disposition that makes it valid.

*And lead us not into temptation.* Words we find difficult to understand. They trouble us.

What troubles and shocks us at first is that the request *lead us not into temptation* logically implies that God can be a tempter, whereas we all know that that is the Devil's work, and St. James's Epistle is there to confirm that "God is not a tempter" (*Non est tentator Deus*).

The answer is that we are faced here with the words of Jesus Christ and all we have to do is endeavor to understand them, not discuss them, much less change them because we cannot see their meaning.

The fact is that God does not lead us into temptation as a bad friend does by evil advice, or as the Devil puts wicked desires into us and shoves us by the shoulders into sin, or as we lead ourselves into temptation when we amuse ourselves and misuse ourselves, we who are our own devils and worst friends. If we are tempted, it is because we are engaged in the external world and torn in the struggle for life.

But God created the world, and nothing is done in it that the Almighty does not will or permit. That is why we do not pray that the Devil not lead us into temptation, but that God not send us the Devil nor send us to him.

The Devil makes two personal appearances in the Scriptures, one in the temptation of Christ in the desert and the other in the Book of Job. In the desert, we see the Son of Man and the Devil struggling with each other, but related and conversing. In the Book of Job, Satan presents himself familiarly before the throne of God, like a King's fool, and God asks him where he has been and how he is. He gives him permission, if not the order, to go and try His servant, the righteous man.

One sees from these examples that the Devil has his office to fill in the economy of creation and Jesus can well make us say directly to God, bypassing his negligible go-between, *Lead us not into temptation.* That is to say, keep us in your bosom which is our shelter from temptation, and do not push us further away. Keep us in inner life and in love of You where temptation becomes impossible. Agonizing hesitation and the tragic conflict between what pleases us and what pleases Him cannot subsist in love of Him, for I cannot have love for someone without immediately loathing what he dislikes. Jesus teaches us, not to ask for strength to triumph in the struggle between good and evil, but to be delivered from the division of good and evil which is already an evil in comparison with divine unity and peace. *Lead us not into temptation.* This appeal is not a call for help on the practical or moral plane, but a call for love on the mystical plane, and therefore troubling, shocking, and incomprehensible to the profane.

It is not an expression of common aspiration, any more than are the other requests in the Lord's Prayer. It rises out of a state we must strive to attain. Common aspiration is to run toward temptation as one goes to a fair or on holiday. What makes the child, sheltered in the bosom of his family, dream of being let loose in the world? Why does the peasant leave his land and hasten to the city, and the small townsman leave his business to go to war, if not that they are tempted by temptation? The truth is that we love nothing so much as to be tempted, for human nature slyly reckons on gain whatever the outcome: on the pleasure of sin if it succumbs, on the exaltation of pride if it proves itself virtuous. But who says wholeheartedly, "Deliver us from evil, and from the struggle which is an evil, and from desire which is an evil, and from the world, and from the Prince of This World, and from outer darkness?"

The prayer does not end here but returns to glorification, at least in the Protestant version, and it is unlikely that they invented the text.

*For Thine is the Kingdom, the power and the glory, forever and ever. Amen.*

When you pray, and above all, when you say the Lord's Prayer, give the words time to come to birth and grow. Fix your attention on them, let their meaning deepen and fill you, then, with your whole being, utter the word and cast it upwards.

Let there be two times in your prayer, a time of becoming aware and entering, a second time of giving. Utter each phrase and repeat it only if you do not yet thoroughly comprehend it, for there is a strong temptation to turn words one has learned into a breathing exercise and recite them as if one were turning a Tibetan prayer wheel. Utter the phrase and wait a moment for it to fill you with its meaning. If some part of the phrase escapes you, repeat it, not for the sake of "much speaking" but in order to understand the few words you have said. In any case, understand that a gift is a present, and prayer a gift, and that one cannot make a present when one is absent. Understand that your prayer is worthless if you are not there. Your exercises have taught you nothing if they have not taught you to be present. So be present at your prayer, present to God in your prayer, present to yourselves in prayer, present yourselves to God by prayer.

## INNER BONDAGE

The inability to be free, or inner bondage, is due to ignorance, fear, and attachment.

First, ignorance of ourselves. It goes without saying that we cannot know ourselves if we do not know who we are, what we are, whence we come, and where we are going: if we not only do not know, but do not seek to know and in addition think we know all about it and never call it in doubt.

## PROPER TRAINING

It is a misfortune for a man to be ill-bred. There are whole generations, whole civilizations of ill-bred people, and ours is a historic example of this state of decadence.

We are a society of louts, wild asses, incapable either of obedience or of self-conduct, and the two things go together.

In modern education, training is reduced to nothingness. Nowadays, a child says or does anything at all under the eyes of his parents, and they let him. This unconcern is sometimes mistakenly looked upon as nonviolence. It is a reaction against the excessive severity of our fathers, and like almost all reactions, a retaliation against excess by contrary excess.

I saw the close of a generation educated with cuffs and the whip. We have all read in pretty nursery tales of the horrifying punishment and torture inflicted upon children, the cat-o'-nine-tails and the dark cellar in which a naughty child was shut up. Indeed, nothing is sadder than to see a child raise its elbow when one makes an affectionate gesture toward it or turns to explain something, and nothing is more hateful than the sight of a man wielding a whip on a horse stuck in the mud, or on a poor dog trembling with its tail between its legs.

Bad training. A well-trained animal is never ill-treated. Any animal trainer, whether he is dealing with a performing flea or a circus horse, puts on show a creature with a glossy coat. He teaches it with flicks of the whiplash and small rewards; he is firm and watchful, but never cruel.

There is no doubt that the best method of training is attention and love. The rider who loves his mount makes it docile to his hand, *mansuetus*,* and at the same time happy to be in the hands of its master.

This form of obedience is an indispensable pattern. What takes place in childhood will recur in the apprenticeship to life and to any craft or profession or art whatever.

There are habits of order, accuracy, and elegance necessary

---

* *Mansuetus: manu suetus*—accustomed to and persuaded by the hand.

in all work. They are part of a man's skill. A craftsman knows how and where to keep his tools. He keeps his workshop clean and arrives on time. His place of work is not a distressing scene of untidiness, slovenliness, dirt, and bad taste, and if he wants to work several hours without interruption as a good worker does, he will certainly go about it with method.

Every master of his profession, whether a laborer or a musician, subjects his body and intelligence to discipline.

There are, then, three degrees in training: training in childhood, apprenticeship in a skill, and lastly, religious practice which, it must be emphasized, is training, a spiritual discipline, the condition on which one can talk of the spirit as something accomplished, concrete, real, and serious, and not vague and illusory.

One of the characteristics of the century is the noise ill-bred people make and their self-importance in regard to spiritual, sublime, and religious matters, philosophy, and the arts. Then, in Nietzsche's words, "The spirit begins to smell." They are masters without ever having been disciples, masters without discipline or disciples. How can one keep precious nectar in a flawed phial? And even if God took the trouble to send a wild ass grace, how could it not be lost like water in sand? Grace will pass right through him and make him kick up his heels more than ever.

For a lightning instant, we shall see in him something like inspiration. But woe unto us if we let ourselves be duped. We shall be disappointed.

For what constitutes capacity is humble discipline.

Capacity is a very strong word. There is no need to say capacity for what. Capacity is the power to receive and contain. A vase is *capable* when it does not leak. An untrained, ill-bred person cannot contain. On the other hand, capacity or ability to contain does not affect the value of the content. Without it, there cannot be content, but if there is no content, capacity cannot replace it.

But there are not only societies of wild asses, detestable because of their disorder, their many pretensions and pretenses, their faithlessness and fickleness, their inconsistency and imbecility, each having it his own way at the expense of others, each out for himself and claiming to be self-sufficient. There are also well-trained societies who are that and no more, societies of performing dogs, circus monkeys, and dancing bears.

To be sure, they are well-bred, obey their countries' laws, and are remarkably credulous, docile in their very reasoning. This stands them in stead of virtue, spirit, worth, and freedom.

There is no human virtue that does not become deadly when it is given too much importance because it is taken for a good in itself and is not kept in its place. On the other hand, we cannot rid ourselves of such an error by committing the error of ridding ourselves of the virtue or esteeming it too little.

It is important to understand that freedom and discipline are interwoven like rushes in a basket. If all the rushes went the same way, you would have no basket, however strong they were. Weave them well. Place them alternately one on top of the other. Learn to establish in yourself the regular alternation of obedience with mastery and you will acquire capacity, or the power to contain.

Let us not fall into the errror of thinking that freedom consists in being lawless, for the good reason that the expression ("being lawless") has no meaning. It is even a contradiction in terms, because law and being are the same thing. For law can be defined as a form of being.

Law is the temporal aspect of form.

I shall try to explain this although it is very simple.

What do you call form? The appearance of a solid object in space? A solid object in space without any form is something you will never find, nor a liquid object either, for that matter. The form of liquid is such that it takes on any shape. It takes the shape of its container when at rest, and the shape of its bed and its current when it flows. Moreover, it has its own color and consistency. It has a mobile, changing shape, or rather, a form that has changing aspects but its form does not change.

There are forms and also transformations, and behind all the transformations there is a form. There are apparent forms and fundamental forms which are the basis of all the possible shapes of an object. But the transition from one shape to another is not without characteristics, and here we pass from space to time, since the transformation takes place in time.

Since it does not take place by chance—and transformations never take place by chance—there is consequently a form of transformation. There is a rule or law of transformation, a law of phenomena, we might say, *a form of phenomena in time.*

If an object moves, in other words, if the change takes place in space, there is also a law of direction, speed, and variation in movement. These are not random either.

All movement, all transformation, all change follow a continuous thread and obey laws perceptible to the intelligence and sometimes entirely or partially intelligible to the senses.

Law is the visible or invisible form of being in time.

When we read that "there is no law" for this or that, it means that the law in question has not been grasped, that it is complicated, broken, and checked by other laws or by the laws of other beings. Poetic imagery is not to be trusted here. Lawless? The movements of a feather in the wind, a dead leaf, a cork on water look disorderly, contradictory, and capricious. But we know that their agitation follows strict and perfectly calculable laws which it is not worth our while to calculate. We know that there is not a movement of the feather in the wind that is not subject to the laws of gravity and the force and direction of the wind, and that there is not a gust of wind that has not a cause.

Their example is that of the extreme opposite of freedom. For not one of the movements of the floating object is caused by an impulse from within itself. Its movement is wholly undergone.

What is freedom fundamentally? Let us seek a universal definition, and try to discover its implications.

Freedom is the manifestation a being makes of its own law. To obey one's own law and, much more than obey, to support and profess one's own law is to be free.

# PART TWO

———

# GOD AND NATURE

## CREDO

*I believe in Thee, God asleep in the stone,*
*dreaming in the tree, aspiring in the beast,*
*loving in man, and dying for that love,*
*piercing the sky with Thy head*
*and passing beyond the light.*

## THE INTERSECTION OF THE CIRCLE
## BY THE STRAIGHT LINE

*. . . et spiritus Dei ferebatur supra aquas. (Gen. 1:2)*

The verb *ferebatur* translates a Hebrew verb which de-
scribes a movement like the beating of wings, a rhythmical
flutter from which waves radiate.

Vibration is the intersection of the circle by the straight
line. It is the circle breaking and twisting because it cannot
contain its radius. It is the circle meeting the straight line
that cuts off its return halfway. The other half swings forward, and the two halves form an S:

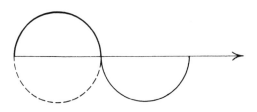

The undulating line or vibration is no doubt the fundamental symbol of the world. For if the circle is the sign of perfection, undulation is semi-perfection, perpetuating itself and becoming fecund because of the flaw in it and the play of opposites. The resemblance between the diagram above and the ancient emblem of Yin and Yang is obvious. Universal vibration returns into the circle:

The Hindus say that Shiva the ascetic created the world by shaking his tambourine, with its two bone clappers which strike now on one side, now the other. Such is creative sound or rhythm. And they define that sound as the vibration of the ether.

But for them ether is not the vague term it is to us. In their philosophy and physics it is a precise concept. *Akásha*, ether, is the fifth element. They add it to the four elements known in Western antiquity.*

## *Of the Quintessence or Form*

Ether, or *Akásha*, is the formal element, the form that is the integrating part of every object, the constitutive and determining principle.

---

* The four elements, Earth, Air, Fire, and Water, cannot be identified with the elements of modern chemistry. They belong to another vision of things. They are not mistaken approximations but, like Yin and Yang, are natural emblems. Thus water is not equal to $H_2O$ but includes the moon, silver, quicksilver, woman, vegetation, and the soul.

In a certain sense, the five elements can be equated with the five states of matter: the solid state—Earth

> the liquid state—Water
> the igneous state—Fire
> the gaseous state—Air
> the radiant state—Ether

The five states of nature determine every being just as the three dimensions of space determine every volume.

It is obvious from the example of fire that the element is not a chemical substance, since everything that burns becomes fire. Similarly, as some physicists affirm, anything hurled at the speed of light would turn into light. The change from solid into liquid and from liquid into gas can commonly be observed. Elements are therefore the various degrees of a body's molecular condensation or expansion.

Just as no body can be contained by a single plane of space, since all bodies have some thickness, so every being partakes to some degree of the five states at the same time. Thus a living body has its part of solid matter in flesh and bone, of liquid in blood and the humors, of gas in the air it breathes, of fire in warmth and vitality, and of luminous ether in its form.

Its form is its light, the face it presents to radiating energy, its own answer to light.

But the form is not a covering, a garment that can be slipped off, and light does not just come and strike it from outside. As air enters the very soul of every breathing creature, so form pushes its roots into the most secret part of every cell. It results from, and expresses, the innermost nature and qualities of the being. *Akásha* is therefore one of the threads with which the cloth of the real is woven, an element of nature.

Light is *Akásha* in its pure state, free and perfect.

Heat, sound, and the other energies are *Akásha* in looser states. Matter is a tangle like a bundle of frizzy fleece. This energy arrested and packed in on itself plays the part of counter-energy. Matter becomes the negative pole of energy. All rhythm has strong and weak beats. Matter is continually traversed by living energy, like the warp by the weft, and the stuff of the world is always being woven. This is right and cannot be otherwise.

## THE LIFE AND THE LIGHT

*Who lives life?*

> *For as the Father hath life in himself; so hath he given to the Son to have life in himself. (John 5:26)*

It is therefore the privilege of the Son, the Word, the Christ, and the distinctive mark of His divinity. But *we* are not, we pass. What is does not pass. Life passes, they say, but it is we who pass through life. Our passage through life we call time. And because we pass through life, we shall lose it. We shall die. But life will not die. It will pass beyond because it dwells beyond. Life cannot die, just as matter, if it exists, cannot cease to exist. Likewise, nothing is lost of what has lived. Life, at least, is not lost. We, the living, are waves on the face of life, and our effacement takes nothing away from life. Life is an immutable mode of being. So what is most peculiarly ours, our very being, our life itself, ourselves, does not belong to us and does not reside in us. Our being belongs to being itself, the life in us belongs to life, we ourselves belong to the Self in Self, God. In Him is the being of all beings. In Him, not in them, in Him is their substance and their seed, their idea, to borrow the term from Plato, who by idea does not mean the abstract image but, on the contrary, the real body of which the things, animals, and people who appear and disappear in this world are only the deformed and empty shadows cast on the wall of a cave.

*In Him, what has been made was life.*

The past indicates that everything that has been made was life to begin with. In other terms, everything that has been made was life before being made. *In principio* means in the beginning. The Latin word *principium* like the Greek word *arche* implies priority, primacy, predominance. Now, this Beginning was (and I am speaking humanly, as St. Paul said, because of the weakness of our flesh) at a time when time was not. Therefore it remains present throughout all time. And the Beginning or Principle will subsist after the world has been destroyed and time consumed. In that Beginning which never began and will never end, in the time which is not a time, in the Principle which is not a place, in the point which is nowhere, which nothing contains, and which contains all things, everything that was made had plenitude of being, exaltation of its being, perceptible to itself: its life. There, all the living creatures who fight, oppress, and devour each other here below were harmoniously blended in the eternal life of the Word. For life, the superabundant overflowing form of being, dwells in the Word, which is the most living substance and the very life of the living God. We distinguish in ourselves Being, Life, and Conscience as three degrees of the same thing because, each being equally infinite, the three together are no greater than any one of them. Being is proper to the Father, Life to the Son who is the Word, and Conscience to the Holy Spirit.

*And the Life was the Light of Men.*

Life is what is most obscure, inward, and silent in being. Its secret cannot be forced or penetrated. Light is what is most manifest, is shed equally over all at every moment, and in an instant invades the whole of space. By passing suddenly from life to Light after placing the life of all things in the Word, the apostle joins extremes in striking manner, uniting the foundation with the summit, depth with height, alpha with omega.

Just as speech is the first, most perfect, and indispensable manifestation of thought, so Light is the first of beings in the world, the first created according to Genesis, the most perfect, complete, and the closest to God. And in all religions, all traditions of wisdom, God appears and makes Himself manifest as Light. I mean that He makes Himself manifest like Light, for nonmanifest, He is night. But beyond the horizon of our sight and conceptions, light and darkness blend. Made manifest in the world, he is first of all Light.

## THE IMPORTANCE OF NAMING

The birth of John the Baptist, the Forerunner, is like that of every man except for the great age of his father and mother. But family and friends and their congratulations and the usual ceremonies are there to make the event an ordinary one.

Then the first born is circumcised and consecrated to the Lord as is customary in Israel since the time of the Patriarchs. But this consecration, a commemorative rite for the family, is of a child who gives it such plenitude of meaning that it seems to have been instituted and prepared for him since the beginning of time. For this reason, his baptism also takes on full significance. Newly circumcised, the child is not given the name that custom and convention dictate, but *his* name, the one given him by God beforehand and announced by the angel in the vision, the name of John, which means God *is gracious*, or *Grace of God*, just as Emmanuel means God *is with us*, and Jesus, *the Saviour*.

So let us think carefully of the name we bear and the names we give our children. For the name is the indication of a destiny and places the bearer in a particular network of protection. At the very moment that Zacharias, obeying the angel, names the infant, his tongue is untied and he sees and speaks the destiny implicit in the name.


## THE MEANING OF THE MAGNIFICAT

Not without cause does the Virgin, in her thanksgiving, repeat the words the Scriptures put into the mouth of Samuel's mother, Anne, who had been saved from sterility by the blessing of Eli and the grace of God, and who consecrated her son to God. This was the Samuel, last of the Judges, by whom David was to be anointed King.

*My heart rejoiceth in the Lord, mine horn is exalted in the Lord, my mouth is opened against mine enemies, because I rejoice in thy salvation.*

*Magnificat anima mea Dominum*, says Mary. We are not

surprised that she has changed the word *heart* into *soul*, for she *is* the soul. By this change of word she makes her own imprint on the ancient phrase, just as she changes *my horn is exalted*, that is to say, my strength and my direction, the horn being the sign of the leader of a flock, into *my spirit hath rejoiced in God my saviour.*

But there is nothing personal or particular in the Virgin. Everything about her concerns essence and has universal significance. Therefore not only the words she borrows but the changes she makes in them are highly important. Indeed, the first three things the Virgin says after the angel's departure form the basis of man's spiritual knowledge.

For the first of her sayings concerns the body; the second, the soul; and the third, the spirit. And traditional science teaches us that man is made of these three elements, that inner man of whom St. Augustine writes, *in interiori homine habitat veritas.* Truth dwells in inner man.

The first thing she says is her answer to the angel when he comes and tells her how *flesh* will conceive the Word and become the bride of the Holy Spirit.

The second and third things she says are the first two verses of the Magnificat. That her *soul* magnifies the Lord and her spirit exults in God her saviour.

Let us return to the first, which touches on one of the basic affirmations of the Gospel (as indeed of all religious teaching): that the body, this "nest of errors and knot of sins," this bag of filth and bundle of pride, this reservoir of blindness and lust must become an instrument of knowledge, a lamp of truth, a channel of salvation, a temple; that it must be assumed by the spirit, transmuted into its substance, and transported into heavenly glory if redemption of the creature is to be achieved.

Whoever denied this could not call himself a Christian,

for if the body were worthless, the Word would have been made flesh for no reason, the sacraments would be pointless, and the dogma of the Resurrection meaningless.

But it is not so much a matter of accepting or rejecting the statement as of understanding it, and the first step is to understand that it is not so easy to understand.

Consider how you speak of the heart when you say that somebody has *heart trouble* and that you love somebody *with all your heart*. You see how on the one hand you know that the heart is an organ of the body and, on the other, that it is a source of noble feeling. In other words, you distinguish between a bodily heart and a spiritual heart. But what is true of the heart is true of the whole body. The natural body comports an invisible body and the latter surpasses the other in the same measure as the seat of courage and love surpasses the blood pump called the heart.

The first error to avoid, then, is to think that the body is just a given mass of corruptible matter. Besides, you know that in seven years' time, not a particle of the matter of which the body is composed will remain, whereas the body remains the same. What makes the body remain the same is its form. This form is not imprinted on it by neighboring forms or by external impacts and accidents, but molds the flesh from within, makes and remakes it night and day. It is like a filter through which matter passes. The form of the body also passes from birth to death, but, rather than a passing, its progress is a continual unfolding. In fact this development, or rather, the cause and law of this development, is the true form of the body.

The body is therefore an active formal principle, which consumes matter it selects from outside itself, draws strength from it, and then rejects it when burned. This formal principle does not result from matter and does not reside in it, but resides in life, that is to say, in the soul. And when the soul withdraws from the body to pass through death onto another plane, it carries with it this formal principle, which weaves it a new body of matter or light, according to the world where the weight of its merits carries it. That is what all the great religions teach with different imagery, yet when all is said and done, differing but slightly. Either they teach that nonpurified souls will be reincarnated on earth, or they assign them to other undetermined places of expiation. That is why religion takes strict maternal care of man's body, and is as much concerned with it as with his soul and his spirit, never neglecting or despising it. Which does not mean that religion does not impose the fortifying medicine of privation on the body, or punishment, a sound proof of love, or that, when the time comes, it does not expose the suffering outer husk to total sacrifice, that supreme honor and aid in our first steps toward the glory of Resurrection.

Now what do we learn from this exchange between the angel and the Virgin? This, in the voice of the angel: that the body can become the dwelling place and spouse of the spirit and the Father's Word.

The preliminary condition that makes this possible is put into words by the Virgin: *I am the handmaid of the Lord.* The body must submit, it must serve, and serve God. It seems to us that our body obeys us and that we lead it where we think fit; that it is an instrument with which we work in this world. In reality, it is the body that leads us to its ends and dictates our desires and direction to us, for it has its reasons that the heart and reason do not know, its own will which it substitutes for ours in our absent moments, and its own intelligence which is stubborn and cunning. Whenever the body is in trouble or danger or need, our great divine soul and its destiny are shaken with anxiety and our intelligence (capable of sublime discoveries) is entirely taken up with finding it shelter and comfort. Almost all man's works, the superhuman work of machines, our colossal social machinery with its tribunals and armies, is engineered only to ensure nourishment, rest, protection, and pleasure for our lord and master, the body.

Reducing this master to the state of servant is therefore no mean undertaking. The ascetic set about it with the patience and boldness required. The ambitious of all kinds endeavor to, knowing that they will acquire invincible power in this world if they succeed.

The first step, then, is to gain power over the body and submit it to our will. The second is to make it serve God and force or persuade it to behave in truth and in charity.

But the body eats, sleeps, and can propagate by copulation. Such is the cycle of its natural actions, which have but little to do with truth or charity, things of the spirit and the soul. The body cannot break its cycle unless it puts itself at the service of the soul and the spirit. But this service, which breaks its cycle and takes away its center, can only be imposed upon the body by force. So the first step is one of struggle and taming. Reason and kindness pull one way, the body and its covetousness pull the other, and man is torn between the two. This lasts as long as the law is external, written, learned, or embodied in someone else's authority. Then the habit of obedience and conformity becomes a need. Habit is said to be second nature. One might say that the habit of virtue builds a second body, a body of righteousness. Blessed are they that hunger and thirst after righteousness. Blessed is he for whom righteousness becomes as pressing as a bodily need, for he proves thereby that he already possesses a spiritual body and will inhabit the kingdom. It sometimes happens that the invisible body thus formed shines through the natural body and emits light, as is represented by the halo of saints. It can also support or raise the body and make it walk upon the waters or fly, and discharge through it power to heal the sick by touch.


# NAMES


Why and how can a name have power and religious validity? While God brings beings to birth by naming them, we humans bring God to birth by invoking Him, for if we had neither *nama* nor *rupa* to hold on to, neither invocation nor image, how could we grasp at the immense truth of God? The name, the word, can be mere currency for exchange, or an instrument for abstract speculation. Thought then uses words as stepping stones, treading on them as briefly and lightly as possible, and making them interchangeable.

But there is another way of using language, which is to take the word as a *memorial*, and by memorial I mean that which fixes an event in memory. The word, the image, or the word-image is the most powerful of all means of condensing thought; and although it may be a means of exchange and therefore of letting thought flow away, it can also become an instrument for arresting, correcting, and deepening it, provided it is properly employed. And every religion without exception employs it in this way.

For a multitude of religions of all countries, all sects, all traditions, ardent invocation of the simple name of God has been the major means of reaching the first word, the key word, the "lost word" or "ineffable name," the silence behind all words where all meanings are one. The name can be the way to silence. It is the instrument of concentration, and while invocation makes God be in us, at the same time it makes us be by condensing us, for the state of self-dispersion is the state of nonbeing. There is no other nonbeing possible, since absolute nonbeing absolutely is not. There is no other manner of not being than self-dispersion, for the self-dispersed is as if he were not. Everything that serves to condense him, gather him in, prevent him from flowing in all directions, and fleeing, fleeing himself and escaping, will make him be. Thus, evoking the name of Being has the power to make us be, and this is the universal use of the mantra which you are beginning to experience in your exercises, since that is exactly how you have learned to use the words of a given formula. The formula is given you in full understanding of your need at the moment of your development. It is stuck into you like a stick into your wheels to stop you on the downward slope, or lit like a fuse the day all your gunpowder is stored up in your cellar. And the word, a word of everyday speech just like any other word you use daily, can spark off an explosion in you, a revolution, a revelation. The God-Word is therefore a name loaded with truth. This way of naming the Second Person of the Trinity is justified by all religious traditions, but it is not the Lord's true name, at least if we are to believe St. John himself. In Revelation 19:12, he tells us, "His eyes were as a flame of fire, and on his head were many crowns; and he had a name written, that no man knew, but he Himself.

"And he was clothed with a vesture dipped in blood: and his name is called The Word of God."

Similarly, in the Egyptian "Book of Truth of Word"* it is written, "I have evoked and proclaimed all His names, save the true name which is known only to Himself."

* Part of the Egyptian *Book of the Dead.*

# TRADITION

At the very moment when Jesus tells the woman of Samaria that the place of worship is neither in Jerusalem nor elsewhere, and professes a religion of the spirit and of truth, that is to say, absolutely universal, He utters these astonishing words: "Ye worship ye know not what; we know what we worship, *for salvation is of the Jews.*" The Jews who condemn the Samaritans! The Jews who will condemn, who have indeed already condemned Christ himself! What can the words mean? This meeting between the Samaritan woman and the Jew has given rise to endless discussion.

But Christ's answer is not as closely concerned with exalting the Chosen People as at first seems. Even if there were no longer a single Jew on the face of the earth today, the answer would still be valid. Translated into the language of today, and into the language of the West, it means roughly this: salvation will not come from founders of small religions who do not know what they worship, any more than from priests of traditional religion who do not know what they worship. *Salvation is of the Jews* might be translated into contemporary speech as *Salvation is of the Catholics.* Salvation will not come from the Samaritans, that is to say, laymen and heretics, founders of sects, false prophets, heterodox masters. It will come from the *orthodox*, those who accept tradition *but understand it.* Throughout His life, Jesus Himself set the example of this submission to traditional teaching. Every year, even at the risk of His life, He went up to Jerusalem at Passover as the law prescribed and went to the Temple as He had when a child. And we are told that His mother sacrificed two turtle doves—the offering of the poor—for His purification.

If the Christian religion has broken away from the Jewish one, it is not by Christ's command, nor by the deliberate will of His disciples, but because the heirs of that tradition drove them out. It was in spite of themselves, so to speak, that they founded another religion which nevertheless claims to be the same, refers to the same holy books and recites the same psalms. Religious reform is pointless, it only multiplies dissension.

## THE KNOWLEDGE THAT IS CONSCIENCE

There are three levels of human evil, and on each of these, three kinds.

Evil exists on the plane of what is merely natural. Our evil is our limitation, the first kind of evil. The second is our flight from ourselves; the third, our attachment to that limitation and that flight. Whereas limitation is what condemns us to suffering and death, we take it for our being. When someone says, "I am this" or "I am that," you will observe that "this" and "that" are not of the substance, but limits. Note this in yourself when you are trying to define what you are. Note that when a man defends himself or fights, it is his defect and his limitation he is defending, not his substance, which has no need of defense.

As for our flight, we flee because our nature is fleeting. Its passing through time condemns us to death. Flight from ourselves is the mainspring of desire and all sensual pleasure. Everything we consider pleasing, everything we call entertainment, everything we desire takes us out of ourselves. We flee and are dispersed like water rushing into a void.

On the plane above this natural evil is the evil properly called sin: willful evil, meddling evil, neither the lowest nor the highest. It consists chiefly in pride, lying, and ignorance. Pride, or satisfaction with our limits. Lying, or spiritual flight, flight from truth. Ignorance or heedlessness, the opposite of innocence. The Hindus, who know what they are talking about when it comes to sin, recognize only one sin: *ignorance*. It is precisely because our morality is the most degenerate ever that we can speak of ignorance as an excuse. Ignorance, and heedlessness, are not attenuating circumstances, but sin itself in all its immensity, all its depth, all its horror. It is, in a way, the sin of sins. Yes, your sin or your crime will be forgiven you if you are heedless, or carried away by passion, or drunk. Your crime will be forgiven you, because it is nothing at all in comparison with your ignorance and your heedlessness, which will not be forgiven. You should not have been heedless, you should not have been ignorant.

The ignorance in question is not not knowing what the capital of Cambodia is or the date of Artaxerxes's birth. The ignorance in question is failure or refusal to know the truth one does *not* learn from others, but learns from oneself. It is refusal or failure to pay constant attention to that truth, to study, and study oneself, to work, and work on oneself in order to enter ever more deeply into the truth every man has within himself when he comes into the world.

There is no need to read books or attend lectures to ask oneself, *Who am I? What have I come to do here? Am I doing what I was destined and called on to do? Am I paying my debt?* Each of us has within himself all the elements and means needed to acquire the knowledge that is conscience.

# THE SOURCE OF LIFE

Is it true that to live is to suffer?

No. Suffering is a hindrance to life.

For the essence of life is joy. It follows that one must not extinguish desire, which is life, but free oneself from hindrance.

But so long as desire is desire for one thing or another, so long as it is turned toward the outer world, it will always meet with hindrance and therefore suffering, for the world is bigger and stronger than we and we cannot extend our limits indefinitely.

So stop pushing, you fool! Turn back. Desire your self.

Go back upstream to the source of life! Bathe there and drink joy.

# EMPTINESS

Nothing! Is there anything bigger, deeper, or more terrifying than nothing?

The whole world is nothing but an immense endeavor to fill the void before which things stop and stiffen into desperate spatial gestures.

Men also do their best in vain. They line up the blocks of their houses and build towns like this. They pile up their campaniles and towers as high as they can to fill the space above.

They raise hymns and prayers with the same intention.

But emptiness falls again, invades every opening, slips behind the back of everything.

So men invent preoccupations, quarrels, and haste, and busy themselves filling as much space as they can. They come and go, go round and round their blocks of houses, up- and downstairs, rush into tetragonal corridors, and shut themselves up in rooms stuffed with hangings and furniture.

And from floor to floor their superimposed and parallel lives repeat one another. From floor to floor, they make love or lie ill in their beds.

## EVERY OBJECT

Every object formed by nature—whether a rose, a shell, a woman, a flame, or a mountain—is a whirl of lines, lines of force come from afar, visible only where they fuse, and shooting back up to the stars.

## BEING AND NOTHING

In God alone do Being and Nothing stand face to face in their purity, in the sense that God is all and Nothing, truly nothing. (If you want to draw a practical conclusion from this truth, make yourself empty and God will fill you.)

Just as God has made the world out of nothing, so Nothing has made its necessary place and relative excellence out of the world.

"Thirty spokes converge in the hub," says Lao Tse the wise. "But it is the hole in the middle that makes the wheel a wheel that turns.

"The potter fashions the clay, but the space inside makes it a vase.

"Can there be a house without a door or a window or a room?

"It is therefore because of its emptiness that a habitation is habitable.

"From being all things come: from nonbeing, their worth."

And again, "Being and Nothingness produce each other."

It seems that in God even Being and Nonbeing do not stand face to face like two strangers, but melt into one, such is the power of divine unity to surpass definition and reconcile extremes.

We say of Him that He is infinite, intemporal, incorporeal, ineffable, and we scarcely perceive that this hymn of glory is made up of negations.

St. Denis says that it is fitting to know Him "by the mode of unknowing," and Tertullian declares, *"Credo quia absurdum."* St. John of the Cross cries, *"Nada! Nada!"** and the Hindus, *"Neti! Neti!"*† Nirvana, and the other "astonishing No's" of Buddha, are only the extreme expression of "negative theology" which is also called mystic theology. And if we were not so ignorant of our own traditions, and especially of the inner experience these doctrines refer to, we should not judge them so lightly.

## THE DIVINE WORD

It is true that speech is closely linked with knowledge and thought, but it is as distinct from them as clothing is from the body or the tool from the craftsman.

However, while the body can go unclad and the crafts-

---

* "Nothing! Nothing!"
† "No! No!"

man live and even work without tools, a thought without any language is impossible. For language serves not only to transmit thought, but also to form it, so that language is the form of thought, its very body rather than its clothing, the limbs of the craftsman rather than the tool.

In the languages of today, so far removed from their origin, there is no necessary connection between the word (that is to say, the sound) and its meaning (the thing). This was not so in Adamic language, whose absolute character is strikingly proved by a sentence which begins in the past of the verb *to be* and ends in the present. "Whatsoever Adam called every living creature, that is the name thereof."

Thus in the primordial tongue, the name of a thing and its being are identical. In Sanskrit, the word *nama* means name and essence, as the word *rupa* means form and substance.

The great sacred languages, Hebrew, Sanskrit, and Chinese, each profess to have inherited Adamic speech and even the divine word by which everything was cast into being.

Magicians claim to possess words which make what they name be, words, signs, and gestures which draw their power from the substance and the spirits hidden under appearance, and enable them to bring about their prodigies and cast their spells.

Poetry and all the arts—and above all liturgy, first among the arts—attempt to recover the operative magic of Adamic speech, which the very animals and the whole of nature ought to understand.

The same thing applies to philosophy and the sciences. They seek "perfect identity" of the object and its definition, but their achievement of this end is forever in the future.

Adam, on the other hand, put into the secret of things by God, hit the mark every time.

That language is a divine gift was known to the Ancients of every tradition. For the last two or three centuries, there have been all kinds of contortions to avoid this truth. But people are beginning to tire. Apparently the French Academy refuses to examine any more theses bearing on the origin of language. It is thought that everything that has been said or will be said on the subject in no way lessens the mystery. We look forward to the day when, for the same reasons, great discoveries concerning the origin of life will be dealt with in the same manner.

## THE SACRED NAME OF GOD

One of the distinctive features of the second chapter of Genesis is that the name of the Creator changes, or rather, that He takes on His true name. This is not given in the Septuagint or the Vulgate.

Hitherto, He has been given one title only: *Elohim,* God, the same word as Allah. *El,* which is an abbreviation meaning impulse and power and the plural, if we respect Hebraic thought, represents the grandeur and variety of His powers.

But the true name (be it hallowed) is of immense metaphysical significance. Written, it is:

*I H V H*

Greek travelers reported that this *H* was pronounced Iaō. Rabbis, who know how to pronounce it but are not al-

lowed to, read it as Iehovah, putting between its consonants
the same vowels as in Adonai or Edonai,

$$I \quad H \quad V \quad H$$
$$E \quad o \quad A\,(i)$$
$$d \quad n$$

which is the same word as Adonis, the God of Resurrection
and Spring who was worshipped in the Phoenician mountains. His name also means the Lord.

The Holy Name in four letters, unpronounceable by for-
eigners, is forbidden to the Jews. His Name is not spoken
lest it be defiled. The High Priest alone, on the occasion of
some solemn feast, cries it out in the secret of the Sanctuary.

Vowels in Semitic languages sound like those in the un-
accentuated syllables of English, such as the *e* in *the*. They
vary according to local pronunciaton. If *e* is given the neutral
sound it has in *her*, what the High Priest probably called
out could be transcribed as

Ye　He　Ve　He

with the *h* pronounced as if blowing into a trumpet.

When I suggested this to a Lithuanian Rabbi who was
also a philologist, he looked at me with astonishment border-
ing on fear. He was scandalized and at the same time dazzled
with admiration that a Goy should have hit the mark. He
told me that the doctors in the Yemen, the most conserva-
tive among the Jews, *dare* pronounce it thus.

So much for the sound, which is of great sacramental and
cosmic importance. Let us now consider its unfathomable
meaning. Every Hebrew letter has intrinsic significance independently of its composition in words. There is no need to
be well versed in the Cabbala to see that the spirit that blows

in the *H* blows from the *Iod* of the Father to the *Vav* of the verb and from there blows on the Prophets, the apostles, and the inspired. This is the meaning of the second *H*.

As for the body of the word, it means "He who is he who is," since it condenses three forms of the verb *to be: I am, I was,* and *I shall be,* in one eternal present.

> *O my soul*
> *Bless the Lord*
> *And from the depth of my being*
> *His Holy Name.*

Or as St. Francis puts it: "No man is fit to utter Thy name."

## FROM FALL TO FALL INTO SALVATION

Here, then, is the fatal moment, the great tragedy of man. Yet there is nothing appalling in the scene, nothing to make our hair stand on end.

Adam's affliction is not a bone-crushing affliction, but simply happiness lost.

One might have expected to see him struck down in his guilt by death, since God had warned him, "The day thou eatest of this fruit, thou shalt surely die." But he keeps his health and all his strength for hundreds of years. Death is only a vague and distant threat.

It would have seemed just if God had deprived him of the intelligence he had so gravely misused, and sent him off to graze with the beasts of the field. On the contrary, He confirms his full possession of it and the almost divine powers it confers (Gen. 3:22).

Nor does He deprive Adam of the freedom which was the occasion of his fall.

Nor of the woman, his accomplice, nor their love.

Perhaps God thinks, "Go away from me right to the end of the road that you have chosen. Keep the gifts you have stolen from me and experience them to the full. When you have suffered enough to understand, you will come back to me."

But to our dreary stupefaction, the Lord God says nothing of the kind. The way to salvation seems as securely barred as the way to the Tree of Life. There seems to be no escape from the state of sin. Death appears to be a total return to dust. God commands nothing, forbids nothing, lays down no law, gives no recommendation, prescribes no rite, makes no allusion to the slightest gleam of hope* or promise of salvation. There is no mention of the soul, or immortality, or resurrection. Nothing but dust returning to dust.

Can the ways of God be fathomed? Can a man speak other than human language? If what I am about to say is senseless, may God forgive me.

In the beginning, did He not destine man only to happiness on earth?

Adam loses that happiness through sin, and falls into a difficult, precarious, and dangerous state. But already in the first generation, his sons learn to offer up sacrifice.

And one of them plunges into crime.

Then come Enoch, the great city, and massive sin, and the Flood. God saves the purest seed of all, blesses it, and seals the first covenant.

Yet crime spreads and accumulates. God chooses Himself

---

* Except that the serpent's head will be crushed by the woman's heel, but that is vague and somewhat negative.

a people from among all others. This people denies and betrays Him.

For every evil, the Lord returns a new good and wider and deeper access to Himself.

He sends men His prophets. They go unheeded or are killed.

At last, when the mass of crime has gone beyond all bounds, God Himself puts on man's flesh and offers Himself up in expiation on the Cross. The unfathomable mystery!

Blessed are they who believe in love beyond belief, in love beyond all measure, and who love with answering love.

## EVE

*And Adam called his wife's name Eve; because she was the mother of all living. (Gen. 3:20)*

The only drop of dew in so much grief and aridity.

In the silence of a landscape bristling with black rock under a livid, sinister sky, this tender word filled with all man's hope: *Heva!* Life!*

It is the last time Adam will *name*, the last time it is given to him to name a living soul. "Whatsoever Adam called every living creature, that is the name thereof." In this name, his "truth of word" returns to him.

You are no longer *Isha* taken out of me, *Ish.*† You are my life enclosed in my depths. You alone can free it from its continuous stifling. You are the Life we want to drink together in this place of exile. O Life! I take you in my arms again, and from our vertiginous fusion will spring the cascade of the living from century to century. We are already

---

* *Havah*—Life (Hebrew).
† *Ish*—Man (Hebrew).

death-stricken, but love is stronger than death. Death has given Life its true name, which is *Love*.*

*H*    *V*

Heva, whom we call Eve. Life!
Hail, woman, lamp of salvation in our night!

## MAN'S INGRATITUDE

Yet from all this something is missing which is rarely noticed, but which one cannot observe without becoming thoughtful.

It is this: our first ancestor is completely lacking in religion.

He receives gift after gift, but is never heard rendering thanks, never seen making a sacrifice, never does he sing praise or murmur a prayer. Never does he turn his eyes toward the Lord God.

His essential knowledge is perhaps a contemplation of the God of Truth in His creatures and in his own heart, but not of God in God.

He feels no lack in himself. The Adamic couple is sufficient unto itself and feels no need.

Their ingratitude, by the way, is quite innocent. They are like those nice children who, because they have everything, think everything their due.

If there had been anyone there to point it out, they would doubtless have been surprised. "Really? Yes, indeed. We never thought of it!"

And this is the place to come back to Genesis 2:15: "And the Lord God took the man, and put him into the garden of Eden to dress it and to keep it."

---

* *Ahava*—Love (Hebrew).

To keep the Paradise of sensuous pleasure.

*To keep* has two meanings: to guard and to preserve.

A guardian must always be on the alert.

Knowledge, conscience, love, happiness—none of these can be kept without watchfulness.

Adam the earthly, the perfect, was so perfectly enclosed in his earthly form that it never crossed his mind to ask where all his good came from.

But Adam! He spoke to you! Who was it?

"Really? Yes, indeed, who was it? It didn't occur to me."

That, perhaps, is why Adam failed to keep his Paradise.


## ADAMIC KNOWLEDGE

*And the Lord God said, It is not good that the man should be alone; I will make him an help meet for him.*

*And out of the ground, the Lord God formed every beast of the field, and every fowl of the air; and brought them unto Adam to see what he would call them: and whatsoever Adam called every living creature, that was the name thereof.*

*And Adam gave names to all cattle, and to the fowl of the air, and to every beast of the field; but for Adam there was not found an help meet for him. (Gen. 2:18–20)*


We were to see Adam at work. Well, here he is!

What work was it? He did not have to work for food since the fruits of the garden sufficed. He did not have to clothe himself, nor build walls, since he had not sinned.

He had only to busy himself with the great undertaking for which he had been created: knowledge.

The great undertaking by which he assimilates all things, equals all things, surpasses all things, and does honor to the divine image and likeness.

The image passively and freely received. "Likeness" actively made. Knowing is entering into connection with Being, coming to birth with the known, being associated in the work of creation.

Thus, when He had formed out of the ground every beast of the field and every fowl of the air, God brought them to Adam and presented them to him to see how he would name them. *Ut videret*. But who is the subject of *ut videret*? God, or Adam?

God who knows all has no need of little experiments "to see how." So this could consequently mean that the All-Knowing presents them to Adam to let him see that he can name them, to show him the marvelous power of knowledge he possesses.

But, you may say, there has never been any question of knowledge except concerning the forbidden tree, which Adam has not yet approached. There has been no mention of *knowing*, but simply of *naming*.

Yes, but how can one name without knowing?

## THE IMAGE AND LIKENESS OF GOD

He was created in the image and likeness of God. Such is his definition and his reason for being.

*Image and likeness*: one of the double terms in which Hebraic eloquence is so rich. Nevertheless, the two words are not quite synonymous.

*Image* is the term which recurs in the second commandment on the table of the law. *Thou shalt not make unto thee any graven image.* And the reason for this prohibition is that the image you might engrave would be a wrong one, and the worship it inspired, wrong worship for the work of your own hands, whereas the true image of the living God is you, a living man such as God created you. It is not the work of the creature, nor the creature himself that must be worshipped, but the Creator alone, unimaginable because immense.

But if God is unimaginable and therefore has no image, how can one say that man is in the image of God?

Man is in God's image insofar as he is invisible and immense, that is to say, in his spirit. Its presence is revealed in his appearance by certain features and signs that the spirit alone can read.

The image is therefore God's imprint on him. In this respect, the whole universe bears the mark of its maker and tells of the wonders of the Lord. *Enarrat mirabilia Domini.* Man, in body as well as in spirit, is also the image of the world.

But *likeness* is something more. It is the ability to give back the image received. The Word of God, the law of God, the reason, meaning, and harmony of things—man is capable of understanding these and making them his own, and of rendering thanks for them as a reflection sends back a sunbeam. Man's intelligence mirrors the glory of God. Such is his reason for being. God's will, to which every being is subject for its great good, is something man is capable of conceiving and of undergoing consciously and freely and thereby he enters the joy of his Lord. Such is his reason for being.

# THE FLAMING SWORD

*So he drove out the man; and he placed at the east of the garden of Eden Cherubims, and a flaming sword which turned every way, to keep the way of the tree of life. (Gen. 3:24)*

We are tempted, like icon painters, to put the flaming sword into a cherub's fist, but the text does not say that. It says "cherubims and a . . . sword," a flaming, whirling, sword to guard the path that leads to life.

For the first time, we see cherubim appear. We have never been told of their creation.

It is also the first time that we hear of fire, at least, of earthly fire, which should perhaps be put into Adam's hand.

The fact is that man's presence is always indicated by fire.

Fire, as we see in the creation of the stars, is the first step in Light's descent into matter.

Light shines and illuminates. It is entirely beautiful and entirely good.

Fire shines too, but burns. It is a two-edged sword.

Which is the exact image of good and evil.

Like intelligence, it is one of God's gifts that man has taken with him into exile, and uses and misuses.

He lights it to light the dark and celebrate his feasts.

He lights it for prayer and sacrifice.

He lights it to comfort himself and keep away the cold and fear of the night.

He lights it to cook his food and give savor to what has none.

He lights it to smelt metal and forge utensils and tools.

He lights it to forge swords to kill his enemy; he lights it to burn down the house and town of his neighbor.

He lights it to do anything at all, which is why it is said that the sword turns every way. It will do anything, including destroy by the backflash of flame. He deserves everything he has made and himself with it.

That is why one after another Babylons have fallen in flame. That is why it is written that the Lord will come and "judge the world by fire."

But the fire will not be in the hand of the Lord nor in the angel's, but in the hand of man.

Once again, let us proclaim it, God does not send evil or death, or even deserved suffering. The path of life is barred to man by the fire in his own hand and the spirit that made of that fire a sword that turns every way.

As for the angel, it is a motionless, transparent figure, the invisible obstacle inherent in immanent justice, against which the sinner stumbles when he wants to reach happiness, peace, and love without first opening his hand and throwing away the sword.

## THE LIVING TRUTH OF THE GOSPELS

The apostle has his reason, and follows a clearly traced, undeviating path toward his end, which is to present to the world the perfect example that alone deserves to be commemorated, to point out the truth, and to preach spiritual revolution not by theories and systems, but in words of life, by a history.

The history is that of the Word made flesh. No fact is recounted which is not a sign and a lesson. It is up to us to grasp its meaning, which the narrator never explains lest he lose touch with the facts, and lose the savor of life. That is why scenes from the life of Jesus strike our senses so vividly and touch us almost bodily. Much more than an account or a representation, they become a presence. How can we doubt what is thus set before us? Yet not a color is named; not a face, not a landmark is described; and here we are, face to face and alone with things.

# BAPTISM

At the end of the stony road runs the river Jordan, the most inhuman of rivers, in its rut of rock. It comes from the snows on Hermon and plunges between two deserts to end up lower than the earth in the salt and bitumen of the Dead Sea basin. It is like a current and link between Heaven and earth, a river of penance.

To enter it, you lay down your bundle and take off your clothes. And John pushes the penitent, stark naked, into the water and presses his head down under the surface with his heavy hand. He holds you down, your breath held in the chill dark until all thought has gone out of you and you long furiously to be free in the air and the light. Then you come out, gleaming and new, stripped not only of your clothing and possessions, but also of your store of habits and the outer husk of your person. That is how John initiates and renews men and sets them free.

And John had his raiment of camel's hair because the camel is the most sober and humble of beasts of burden and kneels down to be loaded and carries its burden right to the end without water or palm trees for great stretches. He had a leathern girdle about his loins because he had complete and all-round control of his desires and appetites. His meat was locusts which, like excited opinion and dangerous fantasy, jump into the air on all sides only to fall to the ground again a little further on. He knew how to lay hands on them, dry them in the sun of truth, grind them down into dust, and feed on their pulp. He knew the taste of the wild honey hidden in holes in the rock, the sweet substance of joy inside the rough and terrible outer crust of things.

## ENERGY AND MATTER

We have already learned to see water as more than the compound defined as $H_2O$. In Verse 2 of the first chapter of Genesis, we learned the name of nothingness; then, in Verse 6, that of the substance which makes the sky and supports light. So much for the waters which were above the firmament.

We must do the same thing now concerning the waters which were under the firmament, and the dry land that comes out of them by separation. Here we have the two substances philosophy and science have taught us to name as the foundation of natural phenomena: energy and matter.

Water, fluid and formless, perpetually moving, is energy. Earth, dry, compact, and inert, is matter.

It should be noted for a start that the text does not present dry land and sea as two juxtaposed objects, but as the two poles of one and the same reality, issuing one from the other. It is just like the separation of the waters above the firmament from those under the firmament. Between them the divine hand has traced a circular and eternal limit named Firmament, a transparent limit between water and water. Likewise, water and earth are of the same water. They are energy and matter, the two faces of the same substance, the strong beat and the weak beat of the same rhythm.

A capital discovery of science in this century was that of the unity of substance, shown by the conversion of matter into energy. It is therefore legitimate to affirm that *everything is energy* and that *Being and Power are the same thing*. This reverses the traditional vision of things and simplifies the system of explanation. We are no longer faced with a world of passive, compact objects set in motion by some unknown external action. Every body is charged with intrinsic energy and constantly traversed, now transported, now transformed by the great free energies that roam the universe like mountain winds. The question is not so much "How is it that things move?" as "How can anything hold still together  long enough to be called a thing?"


## Harder than Matter: Materialism

The discoveries of modern physics have pulverized, emptied, and blasted the very concept of matter.

I am speaking literally.

*Pulverized*, because they have reduced every body to a multitude of particles in perpetual agitation.

*Emptied*, because they have shown that the volume of these particles is infinitely small compared with the distances that separate them.

*Blasted*, because they have given the name of *electron* to the tiniest of material particles, thus recognizing that it is not a grain of matter but an electric spark, a pure load of energy, loaded, so to speak, upon nothing.

Which confirms Shakespeare's statement that "we are such stuff as dreams are made of." One might therefore be excused for imagining that the progress of science has destroyed the very foundations of materialism. Not so!

Science may have succeeded in disintegrating matter in theory as in deed, it has certainly not made old materialism lose a single believer. On the contrary, it has won others over to it.

For materialism does not at all depend on one's image of the structure of bodies. It is a turn of mind. A turn of mind turning against itself and taking itself for a by-product of the blind forces of Outside.

Materialists have existed in every age, although this is the century of their reign. They exist in the East as in the West. (One of the six systems of Hindu philosophy adheres strictly to materialism and atheism.) Some materialists cannot admit to themselves that they are so. Some are churchgoers and priests. With the old materialism, they were afraid of compromising themselves; but the new one (materialism without matter) seduces great numbers of them, for it lends itself more easily to confusing the issue as well as to highly imaginative mystical interpretations.

But to return to matter, what have we said about it? That it does not exist? That it is an illusion of the senses? Or, as the school of philosophy called "idealistic" affirms, that it is a creation of the mind?


## The Absurd Reality of Matter

If our minds had created matter, matter would not so constantly astonish our intelligence or oppose our will in such a terrible way. If our minds had made it, they could remake it. I mean, we could rebuild the world with our eyes closed, starting from a few axioms. Great minds have not failed to make the attempt and their strict logic has led them into some brilliant errors.

Let us grant the philosophers that matter, as it is generally understood—a thing in itself that is and always has been, inert, impenetrable, indestructible, eternal like God, the great mother who gives birth to all things including life and spirit and into whose womb all return—let us grant, then, that this is just an idea, and a singularly obscure and self-contradictory one.

Let us recognize, however, that matter exists independently of any idea; that it *exists* in the original meaning of the word (*sistere* or *stare*—to stand, *ex*—outside). Outside what? Outside the human mind, short of and beyond the limits of human knowledge, the unknown kernel of known things, the residue that always remains when the work of knowledge is ended. Far from being a product of the intelligence, matter presents itself as the contrary of what intelligence can produce, the contrary of relation. Matter is never relation, but only a term. *Term* means starting point and stopping point. Far from being a creation of the mind, it can be considered as the sum and mass of our ignorance.

So let us recognize our limits and its reality beyond them. And since it is impossible that we created it, and still less possible that it created itself, let us admit with the Bible and common sense that it was created by God, or, to put it better still, was *concreated* as St. Thomas Aquinas says. God created energy and concreated matter, just as He concreated darkness by separating it from the light He created. He drew matter out of nothingness and left it full of nothingness as modern science has observed, at the lowest limit of being.

We have said that matter is the reverse side of energy, the weak beat of the rhythm in which energy is the strong beat. This requires explanation.

Matter is the springboard of energy, its indispensable obstacle, as it is also the term of intelligence, its starting and stopping point. Without it, energy would act on nothing, would be nothing.


## Bodies, Knots of Energy

But if everything is energy, what can be an obstacle to energy? Another energy.

Are there several, then? Yes, a whole range of energies has been discovered, from light to cosmic rays, not to mention the vital and spiritual energies which are the subject of another essay. There are energies with different directions and wavelengths, different powers, speeds, and qualities. The ether is interwoven with them, and the ether is not relegated to intersidereal space. It is everywhere, giving each thing its form.*

Wherever two or more energies meet, a body is formed.

Its nature depends on the balance of these energies, which may come from the most distant regions of the universe. They arrest one another in the body, which does not mean that they annul one another. Indeed, their reciprocal arrest determines the body, on which they continue to work and exercise their pressure.

The kind and value of the body depend on the number and quality of the vibrations intercepted in it. On these depend its degree in being and its degree of being.

* Indeed, it is *Akásha* or universal form, a constitutive element of all reality.

The form of a solid is determined by the lines of force projected on its mass and the angle of their incidence.

Every body is an interlacing of active relations, which explains the stellar form of crystals, the resemblance between stars and atoms, and the correspondence of our constitution and destiny to the planets and signs of the zodiac.

Which explains the formidable power contained in the tiniest granule of motionless and massive things. As soon as one of two counterforces that meet in it is deviated, thus liberating each from the other and both from their millenary prison, there is an explosion of force incomparably greater than that of living bodies, from which energy ebbs from day to day until it has all gone.

## FROM LIGHT TO FIRE

*And God said, Let there be light; and there was light.*
*(Gen. 1:3)*

This first light does not come from a luminous source. It is not a result. It is not a phenomenon. It is a substance, the subtle matter in which matter will take a body. It is visible light and invisible light. It is creative vibration, the ether, the Form. It is the space, the void that contains all. It is also the light of men and life. It is the glory of Heaven.

As for the sun, although it is a fine thing and, in St. Francis's words, "bears signification of Thee, Lord," it comes afterwards, three days later, for it is not light, nor the cause of light, but a burning flaw in light. It is the first downward step of light into fire. Lower still, the blazing crust hardens and darkens into the heaviness of things.

## Water and Fire

It is as a sign of fire that the sun makes its appearance on the fourth day, or one might say in chapter four of Creation, between that of vegetation and that of animals and man. Indeed, the first three days are under the sign of water, the last three, under the sign of fire.

The signs of water and fire are the poles of creation called Yin and Yang by the Chinese, the weak and strong beats in the rhythm of creation, the lunar and shadow side and the sunny side, the passive element and the active element, the feminine side and the virile side.

In everything, as in every being and every part of that being, the two principles are present and play with and within each other. This is admirably depicted by the ancient emblem of a half-white, half-black circle, not halved by a brutal straight line, but divided by a sinusoid of which the ends merge into the circumference. The black fish thus formed has a white eye, the white fish a black one, and the fishes intertwine.

When a creature is connected with one of these poles according to its sex, for example, it is not removed from the influence of the other. In its very body and constitution there are marks of the other sex. There is only a predominant influence of the one. The predominance is sometimes slight, and always relative. A thing may be Yin in one respect and Yang in another; Yin in regard to this, Yang in regard to that. It is not always easy to discern the proportion.

The first three days, as I pointed out, are under the sign of water. Read them again, you will find water in almost every line: upon the primordial waters, the spirit of God; the firmament between water and water; earth coming out of the water and vegetation out of the earth (watered earth, it goes without saying).

But now that the hour of animals, ardent, hungry, and devouring, is near, the stage is set with symbols of fire; the sun, which is its eye, accompanied by the moon, which is water to that fire, and stars, which partake of both.

But just as water cannot be missing from the constitution of even the most fiery animals (the nightingale and the lion are always thirsting, says a Spanish proverb), in the same way, fire cannot be absent from moist vegetation, not even from underwater seaweed, for all life is flame.

## The Play of Water and Fire

Fire by its nature rises, but water (unless forced) descends. Fire is red and yellow, water green or blue. If water falls on fire, fire goes out. If fire is the stronger, water turns into vapor and is dispersed. In the world of matter they are irreducible contraries. But life is a mysterious fusion of opposites. Here is a variation on the theme, an extract from my book *Principles and Precepts of the Return to the Obvious*.*

## The Wedding of Fire and Water

Life is a sweet burning.

At the beginning of time, Fire met Water, his enemy. And he joined her in secret love.

---

* Published in New York by Schocken, 1974.

Whence all living creatures were born. First, the plants, wet flames, then we, the sparkling flashes.

Sap and water are flaming water and flowing fire.

Wise fire, tempered with water, which does not consume what it has seized, but composes it; fire that gathers itself up in joy and thinks.

Yes, life is a sweet burning.

And on the same subject, here is an extract from *The Cipher of Things*:*

## The Tree

*Moist, upright, steady flame, upflowing stream,*
*Fire must have thrown away his mask of red,*
*Water let fall her weather-colored gown*
*To fight and kiss beneath the stony earth*
*And there beget this offshoot of dark light,*
*That springs toward the sky with sparkling leaves.*

# THE THREE PLANES OF SUBSTANCE

Christian orthodoxy teaches that the unity of God is trinity.

God is Being.

Throughout the whole of creation, in every creature, the trinity of substance is visible. Its three faces are:

matter, or rather, material energy

life

spirit.

* *Le Chiffre des Choses*, published in Paris by Editions Denoël, 1942.

In spite of what is generally believed, these are not ascending degrees of being but, like the coordinates of space, they are planes meeting at right angles. One cannot be reached from the other except by a breaking off, a change of direction, and conversion.

Knowing nature to the full is determining with exactitude how the three planes intersect, join, and are hinged.

The symmetry of figures, structures, and laws is inversed from one plane to another.

Contrary to current opinion, life is not "a superior state of matter."

A certain author marvels at the "prodigious complexity of the living cell," as if it were the cause of life appearing, whereas it is a consequence, and the work of life. An admirable work indeed, but vulnerable and fragile.

The superior form of material energy is obviously light which, far from being the fruit of a long progress, is the first of created things.

Then comes fire, for all energy lessens into heat. Physicists call this "entropy," a current that carries heaven and earth away toward a sort of universal death.

"The irreversibility of time," says one of them, Jean Thibaut, "is linked with the cosmic tendency toward disorder. The past corresponds to something aesthetically better, a greater regularity in microstructural disposition; the future, to a less harmonious state of creational activity."

It is not in pure light that the body can germinate, nor in the glory of flame that it subsists. Not in the sun or on another star, but on the humble planet earth, encrusted, shut in on itself, and almost extinct. On the lowest rung of degraded energy, heat; on the lowest rung of heat, tepidity; in the lowest stage of matter, rottenness; there is where the body grows, prospers, and rights itself.

Matter begins in the highest of the heavens, in its dazzling form of light. Its descending evolution might be called involution, for it becomes more and more confined in hardness and inertia.

At this point, life adumbrates a movement in the opposite direction. That is why it begins at the lowest degree in a kind of obscure seething and crawling. God is about to populate the various regions of the earth, and also the various stages of perfection, with animal life.

Light and life are associated in the various passages of the Scriptures: "And life was the light of man." They meet like the two extremes of a cyclic movement.

In its turn, another plane meets that of life. It is the return to light or closure of all, spirit.

It is clear that the first two only *appear* and *are* by virtue of the third that contains them, includes them, and casts them out of itself. Therefore the last must be called first.

In fact, it is written that God is spirit.

And again, "In the beginning, God created . . ."

This vision is fairly concordant with that of Sri Aurobindo.* For him as for us, creating is an act of involution. Evolution is a return. Therefore matter appears first because it is exterior and superficial. It is the rind of the fruit; then comes the pulp, or life; lastly, the spirit, the kernel of the fruit, its center and reason for being.

## EVOLUTION: A FORM OF THE CREATIVE ACT

That the world just happened all by itself is far from being a scientific certainty, but it is a power-charged idea, more

* *Divine Life*, vols. III and IV.

powerful than clear, a lyrical vision that carries people away and of which one can say, "Yes, you feel there might be something in that."

What remains true is that all life aspires to height. Every living creature raises itself up on its legs or on its stalk and every conscience aspires to truth.

Nowadays, great numbers of Christians believe in the theory of evolution, and this reversal of the situation has brought with it two advantages: first, they have blunted the weapon of the enemies of their faith; secondly, they have enriched their own faith and quickened their sense of natural reality and "divine life."

For God no longer seems to them like a magician bringing a rabbit out of a hat, or a craftsman hammering in a nail, but rather like the yeast working in a dough, a power that flows into the hollowness of creatures and raises and directs them.

"After all," they say, "is there anything in the Scriptures or in the dogma that contradicts an evolutionary theory of the world? What exception can one take to it so long as it is clear that it is God who foments and guides the evolution by which He draws all things back to Himself?

"What is more, evolution is the form the creative act takes in living matter."

*So shall my word be that goeth forth out of my mouth: it shall not return unto me void, but it shall accomplish that which I please, and it shall prosper in the thing whereto I sent it* (Isa. 55:11).

"The living are the fruit of this return of the Word."

Indeed, there is nothing to be said against this view of things, and this first chapter of Genesis (the generation of Heaven and Earth) illustrates it in a magnificent manner.

There remain some pitfalls to be avoided. First of all,

when one uses an adversary's argument, one must take care not to be seduced by the spirit in which it was originally put forward, and fall into the trap of ambiguous language with unacceptable implications. It would be imprudent to think one can accept the argument without any mental reservations provided one turns it upside down.

As for the theory of evolution, we must discern the limits of its validity. Evolution, like movement in general, is a reality which, according to the law of nature, has its opposite: fixity. What one is entitled to demand of an "exact" science (*exact* is derived from the past participle of a Latin verb meaning *to demand*) is that it should determine the orbit in which a given creature evolves, for each has been endowed with a certain freedom of action, a certain time to live, a certain figure and structure, a certain capacity for evolution.

At every hinge between planes of reality, kingdoms, and species, the presence and action of the Creator are evident. Whoever denies the evidence "is a knave."*

To us, God is Being, and being what He is, He does not pass ". . . in whom is no shadow of variableness or turning," says St. James.

God is also Life, and life animates the fixed structures of being. Here, as elsewhere, Yin plays with Yang, weak beats alternately with strong in the great circle of the unique principle.

* "The man who pretends to be a modest enquirer into the truth of a self-evident thing is a knave," says William Blake.

# THE IMMATERIAL ESSENCE OF THE LIVING BODY

*[The body] is sown in corruption; it is raised in incorruption.*
*(1 Cor. 15:42)*
And further on,
   *Now this I say, brethren, that flesh and blood cannot inherit*
*the kingdom of God; neither doth corruption inherit incorrup-*
*tion. (1 Cor. 15:50)*

To seize the thread that links these two paragraphs in the same epistle, one must distinguish between one kind of body and another, between the body and the flesh.

What is the body? What in it inherits incorruption?

Is the body a mass of matter? If so, it would soon cease to be, or at least to be what it is. For all its flesh is not only corruptible after death, but decomposing at this instant in the perpetual production of its waste. Matter only goes through it. The body swallows it greedily and rejects it with indifference, which is its way of saying, "I am not that."

"What are you, then?"

"I am my form," says the body.

But if the form is like a sieve through which matter passes, leaving behind its chemical energy, the form in turn changes singularly from that of the infant to the old man . . .

Be careful! I said *my form*. I did not say *my image* or *my physical appearance*. The shape one sees is only a small part of visible form, but form is much more than what is visible.

Form is also the innermost structure and character. It is the formative principle which works on every cell and fiber from within. Form is what works, not what it works on, flesh and matter, nor what results from that work (the image and physical appearance).

If it does not belong to matter, what does form belong to, then?

It can only belong to the soul.

## THE FORM OF THE FUTURE

The star called "the Seal of Solomon" is the sign of wisdom.

The perfection of wisdom requires that all its parts should be distinct and connected.

Were the elements in Adam? In man, in his first integrity?

No doubt they were, present but mingled, although the text in its extreme sobriety already indicates the three lines of the composition:

*the body*—form and flesh (of the dust of the *ground* God *formed* him)

*the soul*—and man became a *living soul*

*the spirit*—God breathed into his nostrils the *breath of life*.

But Adam was only the "*forma futuri*," "the figure of him that was to come" (Rom. 5:14).

In him were buried the seeds of truth which study, reflection, works, and discoveries were to foster and distinguish in centuries to come. This is yet another way of understanding the *forma futuri*, the form that the meteor of human genius—that reflection of higher light—will assume as a whole.

"God," says Gregory of Nyssus, "is incomprehensible, but man also, by his spirit, is beyond all knowing" (*De hominis opificio*).

## NAKED AND UNASHAMED

*And they were both naked, the man and his wife, and were not ashamed. (Gen. 2:25)*

From age to age, in new surroundings, in different guises, Adam and Isha meet again and suddenly recognize each other.

They recognize each other by this: they are naked before each other and unashamed.

Even if I have not yet torn your robe open, my eyes have taken in the curve of your hips. Why should you blush, my beloved? "Thou art all fair, my love: there is no spot in thee."*

—See, my beloved, see! I have stolen for thee. I have hidden in my bosom two apples from the Tree of Life! Let my beloved come into his garden and eat his pleasant fruits.

—Truly, she is my garden, the garden I will enter. So great is my love, so great has it made her, that now the whole earth is covered with her. Our father, mother, friends, our home, and our land—we left them all and bade them farewell in gladness of heart. They wept, were dissolved, and vanished.

The walls that close us in are disappearing from sight. Come! There is silence and the angel feigns sleep.

I pushed into a shiver of leaves in a shower of sunbeams.

The hinds stretched out their muzzles to be stroked. A flight of birds astounded us.

* The Song of Solomon.

Big wild beasts brushed past us, leaping, but harmless.

For all devour one another therein but none perishes, and they moan, not from pain but from the outrage of pleasure suffered.

An untrodden path led me to the Garden of Delight, the deep fountain, and I swam in your water. Or was it I who melted and you who swam?

But why are you weeping?

—I weep because in two hours' time, in two weeks or in two months, we shall have to see the four walls that shut us in, everyday things, indifferent faces, and the waves of time and people will drown us again.

—Do not weep. Sleep without fear. For in thirty years' time, three hundred years' time, three thousand, three hundred thousand years' time, we shall find each other again.

We shall recognize each other.

We shall remember.

We shall discover each other in the unalterable amazement of the first days of the world.

## TEN PROGRESSIVE STEPS IN THE KNOWLEDGE-OF-GOOD-AND-EVIL

### *The First Step: Hunting*

Adam, deprived of the fruits of Paradise, has to fall back on the (cultivated) herbs of the field, vegetables, and cereals. The punishment is only that of fatigue. But soon, the Knowledge-of-Good-and-Evil teaches him that one can take more savory nourishment by tearing from the animals (his helpers!) their flesh, similar to his own. And he becomes a hunter.

He does so all the more eagerly as trapmaking, sharpening harpoons, and inventing poisoned arrows are much more pleasant occupations than plowing, and more in keeping with serpentine genius. And so he does his utmost to make nature alien and hostile. Condemned to death himself, he trains for murder, and armed with the hook of intelligence and the venom of learning, he becomes the most cruel and destructive of all harmful beasts.

## The Second Step: War

As the numbers of men increase, the opportunities to clash multiply, at first because of the fields and hunting grounds that have to be defended against raids by neighbors, and the advantages discovered in raiding theirs. They quickly perceive that the most expedient and lucrative of works is war.

## The Third Step: Slavery

The Knowledge-of-Good-and-Evil reveals to man one of its great principles: that it is not so rewarding or so easy to obtain one's living from the earth by means of a tool as from one's neighbor by means of a weapon.

The warring peoples who content themselves with massacring their victims and taking spoil from them are retarded in "knowledge." Intelligent people know that the best booty is man.

The captive whose life we have magnanimously spared is just the man to replace us at useful and "servile" work. More knowing than poor Adam, we have found a way of eating our bread in the sweat of another man's brow.

## *The Fourth Step: Exploitation and Revolt*

Another step in this direction (for we are becoming more and more human and civilized) is to perceive that there is no need to use such bloody means nor go so far afield to find slaves when we can turn any of our fellow citizens into one. We need only lay one of the traps for them called Big Business and assure them their keep in exchange for the work of their days and lives.

The poor, the ignorant, and the unlucky will not fail to rush into it in great numbers. The Big Business starts by being agricultural, and the stratagem consists in cornering all the land so that the native no longer has a foothold on it and is forced to beg for shelter and payment, that is to say, slavery.

But the big mechanized factory is a better trap.

Everything goes fairly well, and even well enough, and the producing machine runs smoothly until the day the slave takes it into his head to acquire "knowledge" and shake off his yoke.

When peasant risings, slave revolt, or proletarian revolution are crushed, oppression becomes heavier. When they succeed, likewise, for then they establish a more mechanical and inhuman structure of relations between the enslaved and their new masters.

## *The Fifth Step: Wealth, Poverty, and Business*

The Knowledge-of-Good-and-Evil takes a considerable step forward the day that from the *sensation of pleasure* one moves up to the *notion of value* and attaches this value to the objects that procure pleasure. It takes another step forward with the measurement of the value by means of objects-signs-number called money. Thereafter, the knowledge becomes an exact objective science.

The application of this science consists in safeguarding oneself from want by accumulating goods. Their accumulation creates want all round. Without costing one's own brow any sweat, this want raises the value of what one possesses, favors exchange, and gives the poor an incentive to work in order to obtain necessities.

Buy the thing from people who don't know what to do with it, and quickly sell it where demand abounds. Play the eager servant or helpful friend of your customers—that is the way to spread opulence and easy happiness.

Well, what's wrong with that? Nothing. It is even very good. The serpent is a very useful animal, civil, and so prettily wrapped in honesty that he disappears.*

## The Sixth Step: Sale of Oneself and Others

However, objects are not the sole object of "the Knowledge." It also deals in people. There is nothing that is not for sale: beauty, talent, virtue, elegance, eloquence, trust, curiosity, vice, ridicule, miracles, and mystery, all are salable and sources of profit. An expert in the Knowledge-of-Good-and-Evil looks upon each and all of his fellow men as prey or obstacle.

---

* The connection between sin and the possession and handling of wealth which all obscurely feel and the Gospel denounces so strongly cannot be explained in a few lines. It is dealt with more fully in chapter 3 of *The Four Scourges.*

This attitude does not necessarily lead to evil actions or outward harm. In spite of being out-and-out amorality, a falsification of all human relations, an "inclination toward evil," distinct from evil while bad in itself, such an attitude is not incompatible with good behavior if it is deemed advantageous to show oneself amiable, honorable, and loyal. It may happen that each, seeking advantage over the other, does others good without meaning to. Making good use of ill-will is the business of legislation. When every man is out for himself and pulls things his way, the threads stretch and cross and the resulting social fabric makes order, the order of this world, an order perfectly foreign to that of justice and love, but necessary, serviceable, and even quite pleasant.

## *The Seventh Step: Compulsion by Law and the Atrocities of Justice*

What enables the pretty game of push-and-pull to go on for some time is the fact that it is subject to rules called the Law of the Country. The law ensures the freedom of the players and confirms their gains. It is made by the winners. There are some clever people who know how to handle it. Law, like everything else, becomes an instrument of profit.

This law is foreign to the justice of the just. St. Paul and Lao Tse agree in seeing it as the support of sin.

The justice of the wise is to render good for good.

The justice of God and the saints is to render good for evil.

The justice of men is to render evil for evil, redoubling evil under pretense of stopping it. Its imposture is to call the evil rendered good.

How can one explain that the groans of tortured men

(among them Christ between the two robbers) have never roused the indignation of good people? That the turn of mind which has made so much horror possible still inspires our judgments and finds expression, on the slightest occasion, among the best of people? How can one explain this delirium of the spirit of justice if not by our common heritage of the state of sin?

## The Eighth Step: Power, or Right of Homicide

People being what they are, the Law of the Country, such as it is, cannot be maintained without the use of force, and force must be in somebody's hands. Power is the power to force people to do what they do not want to do and, if they refuse, to kill them. It is also the power to force them to defend the law at the cost of their lives and to kill if need be.

How could the spirit of lucre fail to grasp this means (so much more powerful than the possession of wealth) to satisfy its desires at the expense of others? And above all, that strongest of desires in a being fallen into separation, the desire to be the focus of all eyes, listened to, adulated, worshipped, feared, envied, "like a god"; in a word, pride?

Rivalry between the powerful and those who covet their power has always been the most common cause of war and bloodshed.

Just as want is the reverse of riches and a consequence of the spirit of lucre, servitude is the reverse of power, which, without the slavish obedience and blind acquiescence of citizens convinced of their duty to submit to it, would be nothing.

## *The Ninth Step: The Height of Progress—The Bomb*

What is this much-vaunted technical knowledge to which our century looks for salvation? This knowledge sold to monied powers and warlords and harnessed to the tasks of lucre and domination? What is this inversion of divine intelligence—inventive research, inspired discovery of the secrets and marvels of creation—twisted to ends of profit? What is it if not the most formidable renewal of Original Sin?

And what is the fruit of all this? The admirable fruit? The fruit by which the nature of the tree is known?

The Bomb.

## *The Tenth Step: Ignorance*

According to St. Thomas, the first consequence of sin is ignorance.

—What? You have just said that it is science!

—The Hindus would reply, Yes: the science of ignorance.

For knowing is grasping the One, the Substance, the Principle, the End, the Meaning of all things, and above all things, God and oneself.

However, in the immense mass of scientific data, this is the only thing lacking. Everything is known except truth.

But is truth what we are seeking? Is it not rather efficiency? But the efficient manipulation of things we do not understand, for the purpose of procuring all kinds of commodities and advantages, results in the derangement of the universe and unforeseeable catastrophe.

## Recapitulation

Morality makes no mention of the Knowledge-of-Good-and-Evil. It knows nothing about it, and to a large extent depends on it unwittingly.

In fact, Original Sin has almost nothing to do with morality.

The reversal of the spirit of truth and love into a spirit of self-indulgence, profit, and power is sin.

Original Sin differs essentially from sins like crime, offense, vice, wickedness, and other moral failings.

Original Sin is intact in clean-living, virtuous men. It is the basis of the highest civic and military virtues, which explains their highly separative and destructive character.

Philosophers, scientists, politicians, and all the Terribly Intelligent People in the world are unaware of it and deny it.

It is so universal that it goes unperceived.

People puddle in it with shrieks of joy or strut in it magnificently.

Cities are built on it, and codes of law and systems.

It is the sin against the spirit which will never be forgiven.

Those who are steeped in it flatter themselves that they have no forgiveness to ask for.

Humanly, it is irreparable, because it attacks the spirit which could alone repair it.

The spirit reversed loses none of its power or virtue. Turned the wrong way, it produces all the more evil the better it works.

# IN THE END, MAN UNMADE . . .

In Buenos Aires one evening, I was a guest in a rabbinic school. We sang psalms, then listened to a preacher. Suddenly, the lights dimmed and a fifteen-year-old boy stood up, put his cap on, and in a loud voice recited the following verses:

*In the end, man unmade the heaven and the earth.*

*And the earth abounded in admirable forms in whom was life, and it turned upon itself in the light, but the spirit of man moved upon the face of the earth brooding fire.*

*And man said, Let there be malice, and there was malice. And man separated malice from innocence and called malice intelligence, and innocence he called stupidity. And he knew how to separate and turn away all things as he listed. And the evening and the morning were the seventh day.*

*And man said, Let there be division between those that are above and those that are beneath, likewise between all the peoples of the earth. And it was so. And he set bounds between one land and another and raised up walls to keep men asunder. And he called the division order. And he saw that order was good. The evening and the morning were the sixth day.*

*Then man said, Let power and riches be heaped up in one place and let need crush the rest and press men to toil. And it was so. And he called the riches that were laid up civilization, and the slaves he called raw material. And he saw that it was good. And man said, Let raw material bring forth riches and let riches bear fruit after its kind. And it was so. The rich took their riches from those who had nothing and the mighty took their might from those who suffered them. And man saw that it was good. The evening and the morning were the fifth day.*

*And man said, Let there be sciences and pharos of malice to light civilization and separate it from the poor in spirit, and let them class and order all natural and human creatures and all things having the breath of life and all things without the breath of life, and let them light each in his ways. And it was so.*

*And man made two great sciences; the greater to lay things bare and give men power over the laws by which they are governed; the lesser and less certain to govern the secret of men's deeds. And he devised a multitude of cunning ways to arm might and serve riches, and laid snares without number to twist the nature of things and make men do his will. And behold! He saw that it was good. And the evening and the morning were the fourth day.*

*The man said: Let might bring forth weapons to defend herself and spread, and let riches bring forth engines and multiply. And he made great vessels to rule over the seas and the deeps thereof, and there were scales on them greater than are the scales on the dragons of the deep. Likewise made he engines to search the space that is above the earth; and they were swifter than the fowl of the air that God had made. And man congratulated himself and cried, Be fruitful and multiply and fill the seas and the earth and the heaven with your encounters and your clashes. The evening and the morning were the third day.*

*Man said, Let the earth be covered with engines swifter and more terrible than are the wild beasts and the serpents*

*that* God *created. And it was so. And the earth was filled
with rolling and creeping engines and engines of haste and
engines of work and engines of war. And man saw that it
was good. Then man said, Now let us make a man in the
image and measure of our might and let him have dominion
over the fish of the sea and the fowl of the air and over the
peoples of the earth and every creeping thing that moveth
upon the earth.*

*And man created man in the image of his might. He
created him in the measure of the might of man. Man and
machine created he them. Then man congratulated himself
and said to them, Be fruitful and multiply, replenish the
earth and subdue it, and have dominion over the fish of the
sea and the fowl of the air and over every living thing that
moveth upon the earth and over every man in whom is a
spark of intelligence and over the crowd and over armies
and over heads of state.*

*And man said to the man he had made, Behold, I give
unto thee all peoples that they may serve thee and be burned
for fire in thine engines. The poor and the innocent I give
unto thee every man of them that thou mayest beat and
force and temper them until they be hardened and do cut
as steel; and that when bitten by the teeth of wheels, they
also may turn and yield profit. And man saw the man he
had made and lo! the man was more beautiful, and greater
and stronger than he, and he fell down with his face upon
the ground and worshipped his image exalted in the measure
of his might and was as nothing before it. And the evening
and the morning were the second day.*

*Thus was consumed the destruction of the heaven and
the earth and man. And there were thunderings and light-
nings in the abyss, and there was a great earthquake, such
as was not since men were upon the earth, so mighty an*

*earthquake and so great. And men were scorched with fire and there arose a black smoke and there was a mighty roaring in the wind. And the earth was without form and void. And the space rested from all the works that man had made in his folly, for his works were no more. There was an evening, but morning was not. There was darkness as on the first day.*

When the young man had finished speaking, an astonished silence fell and heads were bowed in the obscurity.

That was many months ago. I do not remember the oracle word for word, but I think I have lost nothing of its meaning.

## ENVOI

The Commentary is ended. The wrestling by the ford across the brook is almost over. Dawn is breaking, but I will not let Thee go, my thrice holy adversary, until thou hast blessed me!

Nor will I let you, my reader, go until you have forgiven me.

For I have offended you in one way or another. I have attacked your convictions, hurt your delicacy, vexed your kind feelings, mocked and mauled your hopes.

I know what you reproach me with, reader, my brother. It is with passing judgment on our world, a judgment as atrocious as it is unjust. And I know what you are thinking. "It is not true that man's knowledge and art have never produced anything but the Bomb! It is not true that man's knowledge, goodwill, and industry are incapable of forging him a better destiny! From revolution to revolution, from reform to reform, from arrangement to arrangement, we shall certainly end up by delivering people from the misery and threats that weigh upon them!

"It is not true that the world is made up of scoundrels, violent brutes, and beasts of prey. Why," you ask me, "have you not spoken of the great surge of generous inspiration that marks our era?"

I know what your objections are. Many of them have already been made to me, especially concerning *The Four Scourges*, at least they were when people deigned to take that terrible book in earnest. They were also made to me concerning Noah, *An Antediluvian Drama of the Future*,* for which I was much criticized. People bore me a grudge because I did not manage to prevent the Flood.

Well, reader, my brother, do you think it is a pleasure to announce catastrophe and make a nuisance of oneself to everybody?

And do you think it is pleasant to see catastrophe looming on the horizon, and know by what logical necessity it must rain on the just as on the unjust, since the good are bringing it upon us rather more actively than the wicked?


And now, do you know why I announce it?

I shall tell you.

So that it will not happen.

Do you remember the story of Jonah? He had gone, very much against his will, poor man, to announce to the people of Nineveh that they were lost. And his prophecy was so true and so inspired that nothing of the kind happened.

* Published in France by Editions Denoël.

The people of Nineveh repented and were spared their doom.

God grant—I mean, man grant—that my announcements have the same effect!

However, getting rid of the mass of crime the Science-of-Good-and-Evil teaches us to perpetrate requires something other than new and more ingenious schemes of the same science, or arrangements, reforms, and revolutions.

It requires the heartfelt revolution called conversion.

Conversion is turning away from the outside to within. It is the germination of spiritual life.

It is turning things upside down and outside in.

"Unless ye become like little children . . ."

"He that is last shall be first . . ."

"Nicodemus, prince and Doctor in Israel, thou must be born again . . ."

It is turning round and going backwards. Yes, backwards! Not to some point in the past, but further still, to the Principle, the Source, God Himself.

Since Originl Sin turns the spirit upside down, everything must be turned downside up in order to be righted.

Since Original Sin is an appetite for self-indulgence, lucre, and domination, return is through humility, giving, and sacrifice.

In these three words are contained all the law and prophecy. Not only of our fold, but of all other folds.

In these three words are contained the Gospel, which is the good news that the time-honored sin is abolished, the old man buried, and the Kingdom of God at hand.

In these three words are the lesson of the martyrs and the teaching of the sages.

In these three words you have the nonviolence of St.

Martin, St. Francis, Ibrahim Ibn Adham, Fox, Penn, Gandhi, Kimbangu, and King.

In these three words are the Gita, the Dhammapada, Zen, and the tales of the Hassidim.

In these three words, the rise of living souls to meet the quickening spirit.

# PART THREE

---

# SOCIAL REALITY,
# UTOPIA,
# THE KINGDOM OF HEAVEN

# THE FOUR MAN-MADE SCOURGES

Want, slavery, war, and sedition: the four scourges of man's cities and kingdoms since time began.

Passive, the first two. Active, the two others.

Passive, the first two, because they are undergone, not done. They are states of things but not events; chronic evil, endemic in every epoch and every régime, the price, it seems, that must be paid for every civilization.

Active, the other two, because they are prepared, premeditated, and conducted; different, however, from voluntary acts, because of their ineluctable and seemingly fatal character.

The fact is that people make war and revolt because they have undergone want and slavery. The latter two scourges spring from the first two, turn into them again, and aggravate them.

# REFORMERS AND PREACHERS OF MORALS

People concerned about the scourges split into two opposed camps of thought. On the one hand, there are the reformers, for whom the whole trouble originates in a wrong arrangement of society and economy. They maintain that by changing the system, everyone can be assured forever of abundance, freedom, peace, and justice. On the other hand, the preachers of morals affirm that all our evils result from our wickedness and vices, and that changing the system will not enable us to elude the punishment we deserve.

Now it is certain that changing the régime and improving the law without changing men for the better is like sweeping a room without opening a window. The dust raised (or at least what dust you have not swallowed) will settle again where it rose.

It is also certain that if men were wholly good, the worst of systems, slavery, for example, would harm no one. If the master were wise and good, the slave devoted and loving, whom would slavery harm?

On the contrary, if a régime which is excellent because it takes dignity and conscience for granted is applied to people who have no dignity and no conscience, it becomes the source of infinite disorder and proves to be the most suitable for spreading mischief far and wide. The reformers are therefore deceiving themselves if they think that they have found an expedient for saving the world. But that does not prove that the preachers of morality are right, or that they know the remedy.

There can be no doubt that if men were entirely devoid of any virture, and incapable of loyalty, courage, or perseverance, they would be as safe from the two active scourges as, for their great and lasting happiness, monkeys are.

To explain social catastrophe by the immorality of men is to attribute the cause of the tide to the gale that swells the sea. Sins do indeed create innumerable troubles, just as waves make the tide fearsome, but the upheaval of a great mass of water called the tide is of quite another nature and has other causes.

# THE WRATH OF GOD

Universal tradition reveals and repeats that the scourges are the result of the wrath of God. In truth, we shall never find any meaning in these periodical phenomena or gain any benefit from their formidable lesson if, over a self-justifying and self-glorifying world, we cannot read the sign and hear the growl of lasting disapproval.

But beware! The disapproval stems from the righteousness of God, immeasurably beyond the scope of our moral judgments.

And this is where it must be pointed out that there is wrongdoing which morality does not condemn and in which good and wicked alike outdo each other, wrongdoing accepted and approved by all, and by which all profit confusedly. It is with perfect logic and in all justice that the four scourges come as if by chance to confound all men with chastisement.

Morality cannot cry out against such wrongdoing because it is the very mainspring of civilization, whereas morality is simply the reflection in man's conscience of the civilization he deliberately upholds. Only religion can explain the reason for this kind of evil, which is the stuff of custom and law and troubles man's conscience only at odd moments and confusedly because he is too constantly and too completely wrapped up in it to see it. Religion calls this wrongdoing by its name, which is sin.

Nevertheless, religion distinguishes from every moral fault the universal, impersonal, and fundamental Sin which it qualifies as Original, and presents this profound truth in a story which the Terribly Intelligent, with one accord, class as a naïve fable.

## HORROR AND CONTEMPT OF WORK

The reason for war since the age of cave-dwellers has been the horror and contempt of work which stem from this principle of the Science-of-Good-and-Evil: it is not so advantageous for man to draw his sustenance from the earth by means of a tool as from another man by means of a weapon.

To pillage and harvest at one sweep the fruit of several centuries of a whole nation's work is all very well. But most of the plunder goes up in smoke. Now, capture men, and it's all profit. Chain them to work, and all their descendants with them; then we are the victors, and ours are the spoils! Ours the orgies and the games, and one of the games is rushing off to subjugate other people.

Whence slavery.

The only aim, the only gain in slave's work is to do as little of it as possible without being whipped: while for the conqueror, lifelong slavery and hard labor take the form of military obedience.

Thus the work evinced returns and redoubles on both sides. The slave bends his back and crawls until the hour of revolt and revenge, and war springs from the slavery that sprang from war.

Another supplier of slaves is the fear of war.

When the Roman Empire came to an end, free men "recommended themselves" to the man of arms, the lord, for his protection, which he magnanimously granted by putting them to work on his land.

Whence serfdom.

Yet another supplier of slaves: want.

Whence wage earners or democratic serfdom.

Other suppliers: fear of hard work and isolation in the countryside, fear of the uncertainties of independence.

Thus, in late modern times, poor and rich in great number have been seen recommending themselves to the government for protection and slavery.

Anxiety to avoid work and get the neighbor to shoulder it is the origin of endless work aggravated by endless struggle. The aim is no longer to satisfy needs but to outdo the rival. The winner will be entitled to possession. His will be the good things of life while he sets the dispossessed to work.

Then, one day, the workers declare war on the possessors, and their efforts to repulse slavery result in reinforcing power and enforcing slavery.


Finally, horror and contempt of work find their most elaborate expression in the invention of machines as an irresistible means of subjugating the worker, crushing free craftsmanship out of existence, getting rid of the rebellious worker and replacing him, and devouring, then spewing out the submissive. The Science-of-Good-and-Evil teaches man to deliver himself from work by means of the machine, and from life by means of an explosion.


Man's elementary needs are four: bread, clothing, a roof, tools.

To be free of these is at first to reduce them, then to satisfy them by the simplest means: the work of the hands.

God and nature have put between what the mouth asks for and the hands can do such a measured link that the most cunning and difficult readjustments cannot restore it once it has been broken.

Where one man's arms are not enough, the happy necessity arises of coming together and sharing, sharing the work each according to his strength and talents, sharing the fruits of work each according to his needs.

It is no use spending another thousand years scratching our heads and squirming, thinking up new schemes or breaking one another's heads to find another way out: there is no other.

But naughty children pretend to be searching, working, and reflecting while they continue to play.


## ORIGINAL SIN


The Scriptures teach that Adam's sin was the evil of eating of the fruit of the Knowledge-of-Good-and-Evil. It would be simple-minded indeed to find this strange algebraic formula clear. The evil was to eat of the fruit of the Knowledge-of-Good-and-Evil: an equation in which the unknown quantity is represented on each side of the "equal" sign. On one side, the unknown quantity stands alone: The evil was: $(x = \ldots)$. On the other, it is combined with several premises from which deductions must be made to solve the equation and reveal the evil.

*To eat* = to take and degrade in order to reduce to oneself, to incorporate.

*Fruit* = possession and profit.

Therefore, the sin is to have grabbed and degraded knowledge for possession and profit.

Knowledge Adam did indeed possess in its green, living

plenitude, since it was planted, a tree, in the midst of his garden. And God did not forbid him to look at the tree or to seat himself in its shade. But the Tree of Knowledge, raised like a ladder toward Heaven, was made for contemplation and worship, was made for the eyes and not the teeth. The fruit should not have been torn from it, bitten into, and mangled for the use of the belly.

## PLEASURE AND PAIN

Good and Evil present themselves in their raw, living relationship as Pleasure and Pain. Pleasure, to urge life on according to its need, so that it may have more life; Pain, to arrest it on the deadly slopes. Man alone has turned Pleasure and Pain into a science, an art, and a calculation. He alone, offending nature and biting into the fruit, brings about Pleasure and Pain beyond the limits of need, even to the detriment of life, and does his utmost to elude Pain, to the point of falsifying its defensive signals and preventits salutary recurrence.

The pursuit of Pleasure and the flight from Pain are the main reason for the existence of civilizations with their luxury and their delicacy, their frivolity and their agitation, their sciences and their law. The sons of Adam—and Cain —have founded cities in order to settle and wall themselves into this sin about which morality has nothing to say.

# SIN AND CIVILIZATION

The Knowledge-of-Good-and-Evil, speculation on the pleasant, the science of the useful, the subversion of intelligence and its deviation from truth toward convenience, these are the sin into which we are all born. We are reared and educated in it, train ourselves honestly for it, and excel in it "as gods knowing good and evil" according to the serpent's promise. And the counter-nature thus created, spontaneous artifice, deliberate delusion, and indispensable excess, is called civilization.

Man, they say, is composed of a body and a soul, and that suffices to define him such as God made him. Body and soul oppose each other, they say, by way of explaining his virtues and vices.

But between the natural and the spiritual, a third plane makes its appearance: that of the artificial. Let it not be thought unworthy of consideration because it is founded on nothing. There, suspended in his error and vanity, and such as he has made himself since the Fall, is just where man almost entirely exists. For the artificial is the stage on which the human comedy and the drama of history are enacted, the site on which Babel and Paris, New York and Moscow are built.

The third nature, in itself empty, draws its substance from the other two and develops at their expense. By seeking pleasure beyond all reason and beyond organic measure, it manufactures a more exacting and active animality to the detriment of the body's health. Meanwhile, by intellectual curiosity and the pursuit of success, by the exaltation of feeling in the pursuit of happiness, it invents a spirituality to the detriment of the soul's salvation.

Nature elaborated and denatured, spirit degraded and policed amalgamate on this third plane where they no longer contrast, and with the help of education, practice, and habit, end up by getting along with each other.

And this plane is neither on earth nor in Heaven. It is the planks of convention, just a few steps above the ground, on which we play our part in the world of personages. It is our life in the city, where we gratify more or less unreal desires and feel more or less imaginary satisfaction and woe.

The personage, with the name, place, and function that define him, and the clothes that tell his social dignity and cover the body he has put into shame and the shade (where he secretly stuffs and spoils it)—the personage, with his acquired culture and manners and his vanity even more active than his appetites, is thus formed in sin, perpetually wronging nature and in false posture before God.

When Rousseau states that man is naturally good, but that civilization has perverted him, he is usually reproached with ignoring Original Sin. But this is to ignore the link between civilization and that Sin, a link which Rousseau himself certainly did not perceive. When this link has been re-established, his statement, with a little retouching, can be integrated into traditional doctrine, provided that by "naturally good" we mean that he is good insofar as God made him "in His image and likeness," and was good so long as he remained such as God made him, but that he has become perverted to the degree in which he has made himself like a god, fashioned a paradise of his own outside earth and Heaven, and in it builds towers to defy the heavens. And his works are presided over by the Prince of This World, the same that offered Jesus all the kingdoms of the earth, saying, "I have power over all things and give them to whom I will." And Jesus says of this world, "It hateth me because I testify of it that its works are evil."

But to return to nature is not so easy as Jean-Jacques's ingenuous disciples think. Just to leave the city is not enough. For the work of generations has made us thoroughly unnatural and cannot be undone in a day by an external procedure or without supernatural help.

# DRESS

One of the most remarkable results of "Knowledge" is the necessity for dress. Having become one of man's needs, as primordial as his need for food, dress demands almost as much work and worry. Morality makes it a duty for us to be clothed, whereas the Bible reveals it to be the first consequence of Original Sin, even before God's sentence.

On the other hand, common sense invites us to relate the use of clothing to the protection of the body from cold, sun, dirt, and irritating contact. But with what admirable patience we obtain and put up with the opposite result! For clothes make heat more trying and cold more dangerous. By retaining the body's sweat and impurity, they aggravate uncleanliness: by softening skin, bristle, and callosity, they afflict it with the sensitivity of raw flesh, make it vulnerable, and expose it to illness. It is precisely because clothing has created the weakness it compensates that it so often seems necessary. It is just as unhealthy for the human body always to be clothed as for a plant to grow in a cellar.

Thus the rational explanation of the phenomenon turns out to be childish. The Bible gives the true reason when, on the subject of Adam's and Eve's aprons of fig leaves, it makes no mention of the weather but speaks of shame.

Yes, shame and respect of sex, born at the same time of the Knowledge-of-Good-and-Evil, because that knowledge makes the soul false with the for-and-against of contradiction. So now, faced with the signs of sex, it is always troubled and hesitates between delight and disgust, between stupefaction and laughter, and no longer knows whether it adores or execrates.

And, indeed, what is the reason for this organ with a double purpose, made to give life, whence its attraction, made to excrete filth, whence the repugnance it causes?

Clothing gets rid of the opposition by hiding the organ. It turns the impure into a sacred object and makes possible the universal, silent worship named modesty.

Universal morality teaches us that the purpose of clothing is to moderate desire by removing the object of desire from sight. In fact, clothing removes the mean and repulsive aspect of that object in order to heighten its prestige and mystery beyond all proportion. It hides it from sight so as to present it, magnified, to the imagination and thereby drive it into the heart and the blood. Among the civilized, clothing is indeed the most powerful instrument of seduction. Truly man owes to it his intemperance at all times and his distinction as the one fundamentally vicious beast.

But the hide-and-seek of desire and disgust is not the only game in which dress plays an indispensable part. It is just as indispensable in the playacting of modesty and conceit, which is nothing else than civility itself.

Dress belongs to the third plane, that of the artificial, of which it is an essential element. Although it answers no bodily need, it is, on the other hand, so necessary to the personage that without it there is no personage possible, since, without costume or stage setting, there can be no theater.

The need that dress fulfills is *to represent*. The need is that of the personage who cannot be until he has hidden the nudity of his nothingness and displayed what he sets up to be. That is how he satisfies the void that makes do for his soul and which, for that reason, is called vanity.

By hiding away the belly and its foul-smelling functions, clothing gratifies the person with the appearance of an angel or a statue and thus exhibits his foremost pretension, while apparently realizing the serpent's false promise: *Ye shall be as gods.*

It perches the person in his place on the social ladder and dictates the attitudes and responses of the actors who surround him. Each, by the simple fact of presenting himself clothed, announces his titles, honors, and rights, and celebrates the part of authority with which he is *invested*.

Dress is the net society casts over all flesh in order to assume and consume it, in order to "package" it. This explains the contentious, harassing severity with which people pursue the slightest eccentricity of dress, with no need of any code, policeman, or law court, since every citizen not only sets himself up as a judge in these matters but also carries out the sentence. The punishment he inflicts may be laughter and jeering or stoning the culprit to death.

Dress is always a livery, a mark and instrument of slavery, yet not once in history have people revolted against it, and not once will they ever seek to be freed,* for every-

---

* Exception must be made for the sect of the Turlupins in the Middle Ages (who came to a tragic end); also for a Russian sect, that of the Doukhobors, who emigrated to Canada. The Nagda Shivaites live naked in the forests of India, and sometimes come down into the towns.

where, their slavery is voluntary and unconscious, which only makes it all the more binding and oppressive. For dress is not just worn on the skin: it implies certain manners, certain behavior, a certain language, certain reactions and certain prejudices, certain "personal opinions," certain habits that have become "second nature"; and by these it wins complete possession of man, who ends up by forgetting his own soul and even his body and emptying all his substance into his mask. And when man is alienated to the point of mistaking his person for himself, the Prince of This World holds the strings, and in his parades and battles maneuvers him at will.

## SPEED

The main goal of "progress" is to accelerate transport and communication more and more. This is a goal such as players set themselves, in itself insignificant and void, like throwing balls into holes: a goal which, at its best, serves only to permit play. In fact, the speed gained serves the development of commerce, apart from which it serves no one and nothing.

Proof of this is not hard to find: the countries where people go to the greatest trouble, take the greatest risks, and undertake the heaviest expense in order to procure time-saving machines, are precisely those where everybody is always in a hurry or late, and where haggard, hunted-looking people tell you they have no time. They look as if they did not know what is happening to them. Yet it is not difficult to understand. Time and speed are not objects or riches that can be heaped up, and above all, they cannot be possessed in common. Time is a measure, a relation, and of relative reality. If I have a car and gain time, it can only be in relation to those who go on foot. If everybody drives a car, I gain nothing. When traffic as a whole speeds up, whoever walks at a normal pace might as well have had his legs amputated. Far from saving time, general acceleration cuts time short, not to mention all the time lost in forging and repairing the machines-for-catching-up-on-time.

One of Andersen's tales that we enjoyed as children could teach us a lesson today. It is the story of the child to whom the wicked fairy brought her gift: the ball of the string of his time, an admirable plaything the possession of which made him almost the equal of the gods. Whenever he was hungry or sleepy, he had only to pull the string to find himself at table or in bed. Whenever he felt ill, he pulled and felt well. Whenever he wanted anything, he pulled and it came. He pulled off his childhood years for fun and to avoid the cane, grammar, and arithmetic. As a young man, he pulled frantically to rid himself of lovesickness and heartache. He resolutely pulled beyond the worries of middle age and business, then pulled faster and faster as pleasure became more rare.

In a few weeks' time, he perceived that he had grown old and decrepit. To his horror, he became aware that the fairy had mocked him. He bitterly regretted things past, but there is no turning back! So great was his anguish that he saw no other escape than to pull the thread. Which he did, and died.

And that is just what we do with our machines, our strings to bypass toil and speed up time.

To say that the advantage of all this rushing is nil would be an understatement. It has been clearly established that the resulting perturbation is profound, the losses immense, the dangers deadly. When a whole civilization exhausts itself going round in circles faster and faster, grinding emptiness, emptying itself of its substance to transform it into speed, and starts to celebrate its fever as a sign of health, then it has gone mad and is rushing toward the abyss.

What is noticeable in the first instance is that these ear-splitting gasoline machines, this noisy and noisome merry-go-round, these toboggans and rockets for projecting speed fanciers to the four corners of the earth, have all the characteristics of the rattle.

They are said to be economical, which is mockery, since they are ruinous. They are said to be practical, which is yet another lie, for they obstruct, collide, and crash into one another. In peacetime and on holidays, they kill and mutilate more people than a war.

They drive as many people mad as alcohol does. In America, ahead of us in all things, there are already 10 million neurotics, enough to fill an asylum with three times more inmates than the population of Paris.

But their great advantage is that they divert, pull the mind outwards, shine, make a din, and kill time.

And the unanimous, furious refusal to listen to any talk tending to turn men away from machines is due above all to their childish attachment to playthings and their neurotic passion for games.

# THE WISDOM OF ARTS AND CRAFTS

Work is indeed chastisement for sin, but the reason for chastisement is purification. Work is two-sided: on the one hand, to work is to seek profit and undergo the consequences of sin; on the other hand, it is to obey the Creator and in a certain manner cooperate with Him by mastering, testing, training, perfecting, and expressing oneself, in short, serving the human family in its common need.

This is what made a craft a possible school for spiritual initiation, because of the teaching that accompanied apprenticeship, the rules concerning behavior in the workshop or on the site of work, the religious rites and observance, and the vows that bound the members of the guilds one to another.

Although a craft was of inferior degree, being more than half engaged in the world, it also required considerable knowledge and depth, particularly that craft whose name means prince of the crafts: Architecture.*

A princely craft indeed, because of the number of workmen and the diversity of the creations it governs, and also because it transmutes the useful into beauty, thought, and worship. Its main task is to build temples "in the likeness of the sky in all its proportions," and to transcribe the cries, tears, and blood of popular legend, as well as the numbers and emblems of occult philosophy, into the long-lasting language of stone. Royal, too, because every craftsman undergoes its law, named style, when he fashions an object whose proportions speak, whose ornamentation sings or

---

* *Arche* means principal or prince; *teche* means craft.

teaches or testifies, whether that object be a basin or a harness or a clog. It is touching to observe that the most difficult and delicate half of human work consists in decorating (a word that means doing honor to) work, which is nearly always badly paid, if paid at all. And for what use? So that whoever rests his hands or eyes on the object will find in it an unfailing reminder of his origin, his destiny, and the road to salvation: the sun, the moon, and the Cross.

## WORK

It is the Knowledge-of-Good-and-Evil that has turned man's work into chastisement. In the divine order of things, this is not so: work is no more chastisement than knowledge is sin, but he should not have eaten the fruit.

Work was instituted in the joy of Paradise, God having given man a garden *"ut operaret"* (Gen. 1), so that he might till and tend it, and by his work take part in creation, which is the strongest joy of love. But this work of Adam's was done in harmony and peace as a gift of charity toward the earth and an offering to Heaven. In the midst of the garden, he nursed the Tree of Knowledge to make it blossom and mingle its branches with those of the Tree of Life, so that it might have been called the Tree of the Knowledge of Life. And Adam, in marveling awe, watched it rise like a hymn.

But by plucking and biting the fruit, by eating it in order to seize knowledge for himself and grow, he not only severed the fruit from the tree but severed himself from the rest of creation, violating divine order. By this separation, he diminished himself. By taking into his diminished self knowledge too great for him, he lost his native balance and toppled into anxiety and restlessness. Anxiety and restlessness bred that multiplication of needs, covetousness, curiosity, and vanity which enslave him in tasks without number or end. And that is how he has managed to make work his punishment and his chain.

Artists alone have preserved some memory of Adam's work before the Fall: they cultivate the garden of perception for its own sake and for the joy of giving, doing no harm to any creature whatever, obedient to the laws of nature and spiritual inspiration. The sentence falls on all other workers insofar as they turn toward the useful at the expense of beauty.

Knowledge in Paradise was living knowledge of the One. Adam, by snatching the fruit from the tree, made knowledge separate and double: Knowledge-of-Good-and-Evil, of True and False, of Beautiful and Ugly, of Subject and Object, knowledge that is external and made up of opposition.

Likewise, his work has become a work of separation and opposition. The most separate of all beings, the one that wants to grab everything, taste everything, poke and pry into everything, skin everything, domineer over everything, and know everything, is in consequence self-condemned to hard, thankless, and violent toil, toil that consists in turning the tender-leaved tree into a wooden post, deep forest into a plowed field, leaping and flying creatures into meat. Tearing, splitting, twisting, beating, boring, pegging, forcing, denaturing, shelling, desiccating, crushing, grinding, and cooking are his work now. Whether it be the plowman's coulter, the butcher's knife, the woodcutter's ax, the blacksmith's hammer, or the soldier's sword, a tool and a weapon are of the same metal. War is work of a kind and useful work is war waged on the whole of nature.

# SLEEP

Sleep is a need which only needs itself to be satisfied. A tired animal lies down on the ground and falls asleep. But what would be the use of being so clever if we could not find a way, if not of adding to sleep, at least of exerting ourselves around it? For this purpose we have had to produce the astonishing apparatus with springs called a bed, as well as the room that guards it, stuffed with furniture and curtains, with its thick walls, its doors with locks, its glass-paned windows, its shutters to protect us from rain, wind, animals, and thieves. Thus, by a trick of the intelligence, we manage to make our rest cost us almost as much fatigue as our pleasures cost us trouble.

# CONVENIENCE

We connect sleep with all the conveniences and softness with which our sloth likes to be surrounded, but this is nothing to the whirlwind we are finally caught up in because of our care to save ourselves fatigue. For in order to avoid a few light tasks such as lighting a lamp or a fire, or going from place to place, or from one floor to another on foot, it is obvious that thousands of men must sweat and toil at the bottom of mines, or in factories amid hellish noise and smoke. The slight relief afforded us is therefore only a shifting of the formidable load, a shift that knocks the scales of justice off balance and will bring the wrath of Heaven upon us.

So true is it that the Knowledge-of-Good-and-Evil into which we have bitten makes us seek good to find evil.

# FOOD

Alone of all the animals, a man exposed on the face of the earth can find no food there. The grasses, acorns, seeds, and roots with which other living creatures content themselves to him are so many brambles and thorns.

It is the sentence that weighs on the descendants of Adam. They have been sentenced to inability not to eat too well, a ridiculous punishment, yet one that causes them fatigue and constraint, danger and catastrophe beyond reckoning.

Yet it is not by his inner bodily structure that man differs from other animals, but by his mental disposition, by the immense curiosity of his taste forever in quest of new and rare things, and this makes the common things at hand disgusting to him and, in the end, harmful.

By applying the Knowledge-of-Good-and-Evil from the outset to the most natural of needs, he first widened that need to a gulf, all the more to enjoy fulfilling it, then perverted, stimulated, and pampered the organs of taste until organic fatigue enfeebled them.

The worldwide custom of eating only cooked, salted, and seasoned food has made the most natural of needs dependent on artifice and, except when it is a treatment for illness, has turned it into a vicious habit. Habit makes the pleasant perversion an enslaving necessity and a sickness that requires to be nursed.

But the earth does not yield this quantity and variety

of food without being forced. So man forces her in the sweat of his brow and is condemned to hard labor from generation to generation. Now, work requires method, calculation, invention, and learning, and so the divine intelligence is harnessed to the task of multiplying obscure, base, frequently repeated pleasure, and that is how knowledge and the fruit *are eaten.*

## DRINK

But there is an even more elementary need of which man has made a monstrous caprice. The cunning displayed here is much more remarkable, for he has succeeded in making waters of fire that excite thirst instead of quenching it.

## KNOWLEDGE

Nevertheless, all through the strange adventure, hardship, and tribulation into which it has led them, knowledge has remained men's most faithful companion, the best of all their goods, the source of all others, and their strongest strength. Knowledge has made men combine their efforts to avoid danger and overcome obstacles, eliminate loss and increase results. It has armed them with tools and weapons, taught them tactics and techniques, and safeguarded their royalty even in exile.

The very least chastisement Adam might have expected would have been God's taking back the knowledge he had stolen. But the Lord, profound and discreet in His justice, confirms Adam's full possession of it, saying, "Lo, he is become like one of us, knowing good and evil." And instead of depriving him of this spark of Himself abusively obtained, He leaves him free to aggravate the abuse as he likes and experience its consequences until he has reached understanding, changed his way, or destroyed himself.

However soiled the usurper's soul may be, however questionable his deeds and misdeeds, his knowledge is in no way defiled: it keeps the purity and limitless power of a divine thing. Only its direction is wrong. Even when harnessed to the basest tasks, it gives the seeker the key of things, puts into his hands the secrets of God's creatures, opens gateways into the hidden order of the world, and proves the truth of man's discoveries by the efficiency of their results.

## WISDOM

Moreover, it must be acknowledged that humanity has not in all things and always betrayed God's trust in it: there have always been men who have looked on the knowledge snatched from God as the surest means of reuniting us with Him.

Such were the ancient masters, wandering philosophers, solitary ascetics, priest-kings like Melchisedek, acquainted with the major mysteries of divine essence and the destiny of the soul, as well as with the minor mysteries of substances and causes, these cyclic revolutions called Nature or History.

Thanks to the sages, the primordial truths of the first revelation have been maintained in every human tradition.

Thanks to them, the link has never been broken between the world, in its bonds of error and woe, and God, from whose truth it draws its being and from whom it turned away until Knowledge, the Logos, the Word became incarnate for the redemption of sinners.

The sense of profit being the cause of Original Sin—that wrong direction given to knowledge—it is necessarily the distinctive character of pure knowledge always to steer in the opposite direction, toward sacrifice. What is more, it institutes sacrifice, and thus establishes the principle of all religion. It is the hidden kernel of the religions.

It is sacred, that is to say, detached and secret. It is the sheet anchor of salvation and a way out from the evils of the world because it is totally foreign to the world's ambition and covetousness.

Nothing could be more important, then, than to keep knowledge in its purity and, to this end, keep it out of reach of the impure. Now, every man is impure by nature and by birth so long as he has not been purified, prepared, separated from the common current, and consecrated. That is why, at the heart of every civilization, a clergy has been set up to watch over this most precious of man's treasures.

It is not in defense of privilege that it is formed of tightly closed castes, exclusive schools, and severe orders, but to answer the need that brought it into being.

Now, man entered knowledge without having proved himself, and the first proof demanded was that he had not come to science in order to take, but in order wholly to give himself. No man entered without adopting a rigorous rule of life and taking vows and oaths that bound him until the hour of his death.

As for the knowledge to which the disciple gave his whole being, he had to take it *whole*. It was forbidden to dismember science and mutilate his own understanding by choosing one branch of it to cultivate apart as his talent pleased. For knowledge was one, and living. It had a single object: the living unity hidden behind the "I" of each and everyone who knows. But since all things possess hidden unity, and God is unity itself, self-knowledge leads to inner knowledge of all things.

This knowledge, in which the knower and the known are the same, works on the man it inhabits and transforms him to his very depths. It is not a sum of notions, but a source of virtues; it is not only science, but also conscience and wisdom. The man who is wholly foreign to such knowledge remains in outer darkness even if his intellect works to perfection; and even if he is guilty of no crime, he is wholly steeped in sin.

To accuse the priestly castes of having deliberately kept the people ignorant is to pass foolish judgment on the judgment of the wise. They knew beforehand that to transmit knowledge such as they had received it to people who accepted neither its conditions nor its consequences was a sheer impossibility. But in as great measure, and as many forms as it could be received, truth gradually spread, for the nature of light is to radiate. And everything profound and meaningful to be found in ancient civilizations reveals that the measure was large and its forms beautiful. At their origin, solemn feasts were a representation of truth for all the people, veiled but brilliant enlightenment. Family rites brought it into the privacy of the humblest homes and implanted it in the hearts of children. Poems and myths spread its mighty imagery abroad. But it was through arts and crafts that this truth had its greatest effect on the common man, the man of flesh and desire.

# PLAY AND WAR

While play is often sham work, as absorbing, as unproductive, most trades and business, particularly the most honored and lucrative, are sham games, devoid of innocence or pleasure.

The first, most hazardous, and most glorious of these games (if not the most profitable to the players) is beyond all doubt that of war and the military arts.

Just as games are mock combat, so war is a mock game. By mock I mean that it is sometimes taken for useful work from which happy results may be expected.

War is a more exalting game than hunting, and more intriguing than chess, as our grandfathers knew, but people of today have forgotten.

Those who do not enjoy it have set about discovering reasonable causes for it and have succeeded in finding some in the "economic needs of the nations."

And, indeed, in the days when victory entailed the enslavement of the vanquished and the distribution of booty, women, and land to the soldiers and citizens of the conquering nation, war (apart from the risk of defeat) appeared to be an irreproachable economic undertaking. At least, that was how it looked at first sight. But Rome, which had conquered the world by this method, brought about her own downfall, since her sons left their bones in far-off expeditions while affranchised slaves or barbarian mercenaries occupied their places in the Forum and the Palatinate.

For as soon as military brutality combines with civil prudence and legal scruples, war becomes an unprofitable operation. In his famous analysis, *The Great Illusion,*

Norman Angell proves by reference to the figures that modern warfare is waged at the expense of the conquerors, and that every annexation, even colonial occupation, far from enriching a nation, puts it into the red.

It is strange that people have so often failed to perceive that the extension of a state brings no profit to its citizens. Were this not so, the citizens of small states like Switzerland or Sweden would be the most wretched of men. As for those of the Republic of San Marino, they would perpetually be struggling in the throes of suffocation, while the subjects of big states like Russia, China, or India would be reveling in plenty and splendor.

It follows that if nations, even today, are still striving to widen their frontiers, it is not because they are seeking their own interest but because they are interested in the game. Every game has a conventional goal, for example, throwing this ball into that hole. The heroes who have managed to widen the frontiers of their countries feel satisfaction comparable to that of a team of athletes who have made the ball go into the hole. This satisfaction, and the noise of applause, make them forget that they have done nothing good and that their entire gain is that a ball has gained a hole.

Not that war is waged for pleasure or in a disinterested fashion. Nations rush into it with furious ambition (the ambition, by the way, is always puerile and always disappointed), following twisted (and incidentally absurd) calculation. In the same way, the clients of gaming houses go to their ruin, not out of generosity but because of their greed of gain.

But this game is a vice. War is the Great Public Vice that consists in playing with the blood of man.

Nothing as serious as hunger can explain war. Were it

so, the most famished peoples, the Hindus, for example, would not also be the most peaceful, whereas those who prepare and trigger off world wars are the wealthiest of all, so fatly endowed with land, gold, and industry that they seem to be overflowing rather than looking for new resources.

Nothing as reasonable as need causes war. Work suffices. If need be, there are always more expedient and reliable arrangements than the luck of arms.

No, it is not need that causes war, but excess, wanting to outdo the neighbor, the pleasure of trampling upon a fellow creature, the sin of having too much, which makes one lose all sense of limit and go mad with craving for more, the mania always to be right. No part of all that is necessity. It is excitement roused by excess, the folly of play.

Nothing as natural as hatred is the cause of war. Hereditary enemies may esteem and admire each other, as was once the rule, or not know each other at all before they set off to embrace and mingle their blood on the battlefield. Hatred is never anything other than a consequence of war's atrocity and it most affects noncombatants.

It is likewise a mistake to think that the fighters are necessarily animated by love of the Fatherland or a sense of duty or the spirit of sacrifice. The fiercest and most valorous are sometimes mercenaries who are indifferent to the cause they are serving. They are merely carried away by the game.

It is a perpetual wonder that decent young men, kind fathers, devout and charitable churchgoers, commit all kinds of murder and devastation with self-complacency as soon as they get into a uniform. What has come over them to explain such a reversal? The suspension of conscience proper to the player.

Point out to children that the four lined-up chairs in

which they are playing at trains are chairs, that their feet are not wheels and the floor is not a railway—they will grant you your chairs, then climb into their train, blow the whistle, and thunder off full steam. In the same way, if a soldier reflects, he will recognize that the enemy is a man like himself, a good man who longs for his children and home: it is as plain as that a chair is a chair. However, as soon as the good man appears on the horizon, he takes aim at him, just as at a clay pipe in a fair booth. Before killing him, he has emptied him of his humanity as the game requires.

That is how so many cool and cheerful crimes are perpetrated without there being any criminals. Leaders act in the name of a blind people and automatic laws. The people act on orders from their leaders. Who is responsible? The great systematic irresponsibility and deliberate thoughtlessness of the players.

## THE POLITICAL GAME

I shall not speak of Diplomats, those sly and amiable peacetime warriors, public card and chess players, nor of their clandestine brothers, Spies, those licensed tricksters, but shall move on to the second species of mock game, the great society game called Politics.

In the days of Kings, this game was the privilege of a closed and particularly turbulent and corrupt society, the court. They elbowed one another for office, prebends, sinecures, titles, and pensions, and made their way by flattery, slander, conspiracy, and amatory intrigue.

Now that the street has come into the court and the mob is sovereign, the privilege of turbulence and corruption has been extended far and wide. The mask of surface elegance and politeness has fallen, but hypocrisy lives on. Lying has become more insolent, toadying more blatant because of the vulgarity of the new tyrant. Ambition, jealousy, and envy have swollen with the number.

Politics is now a regulated game for which teams train. These teams are called parties and are distinguishable by the colors they display or the place they occupy in the circus where they fight.

Meanwhile, the spectators in their millions, whole nations of them, all hopping mad, howl, boo, lay bets, and double the stakes on their favorites or the likely winners. The crossfire of opinions heats their brains and their stuffed heads explode. The city, and even the countryside, shake with their agitation, which unsettles factories and workshops, splits houses in two, and scratches ancient rancor until it draws blood. Simple souls swell and fester with factitious prejudice and artificial hate. War has to do its utmost, at the very last minute, to bring about their sacred union, union in common execration, and goad them toward another form of diversion.

## PLAY AND COMMERCE

The third kind of mock game is known by the name of Commerce. The speediest and most condensed game of this type is doubtless the stockmarket, speculation on the exchange, which does not at all differ from games of chance, particularly those in which a man stakes his wife's honor or his children's heritage.

However, up to a certain point, all merchants speculate

on stock value, since between the cost of a thing, which is the measure of the labor that went into producing it, and its price, which is the measure of the desire to possess it, there subsists variable tension which is the mainspring of all commercial traffic. Without bringing any new riches into the world, the merchant draws his from exchange. He plays with the fruit of other men's work.

Real work underlies the mock game of Commerce, namely, the conveyance and distribution of goods. But this useful work, and fair and modest payment for it, are of such little interest to the dealer that he usually gets other people to do it while he devotes himself to cunning speculation which will gain him a *fortune* (a word that means chance and implies that it is indeed won through gaming).

The dealer will maintain that he works, that from dawn till dusk he is occupied, preoccupied, and overtasked. But runners also give themselves more to do than fullers, and footballers more than plowmen.

According to the rule of play, and contrary to the rule of work, the dealer acts against all other dealers. The game consists in putting some better-looking article on the market at a lower price before anyone else does, and in thus winning a race which is actually called Competition.

By multiplying human contact and imports from abroad, by fostering pleasure, convenience, and curiosity of all kinds, Commerce is an active factor of civilization, or at least of a certain type of civilization which we are tempted to think the only one, seeing that it is ours as it was that of ancient Greece and Renaissance Italy. But these were profane and external civilizations, quick to ripen and quick to rot, quite unlike the ancient and mysterious cultures of China, India, and Egypt, which were founded not on play, but on ritual.

Commerce presupposes freedom, which it also introduces and develops. Let there be no mistake: its freedom is that of free play, not of free will, still less of the deliverance known to saints and sages. It is freedom of enterprise, without which commerce would suffocate; freedom of morals, because strict and sober morality hamper it, whereas loose morals put it at its ease. Freethinking and tolerance, because thought is of little account to the tradesman, who neither knows the absolute nor wants to know it, and has no use for truth, but likes truths, and the interplay and shock of conflicting truths. Therefore all commercial civilizations mock and sap the revelations of faith but hold sacred the opinions of each and any.

Commerce is sometimes accompanied by a rich flowering of the arts, provided that the arts it favors supply costly objects for sale, and yet another form of diversion. Provided, also, that they forget their original, fundamental dignity, their magic, prophetic, and ritual value.

Commerce is an active factor of corruption, and the development of the one always entails an aggravation of the other, because it spreads far and wide the poison of rivalry, the falsification of products and values, the fever of agitation, the display and turning to profit of all things, and the prostitution of conscience.

Commerce, especially in troublous times (when it prospers all the more), enriches so many vulgar and uneducated people suddenly and haphazardly that the ranks of the society they have forced break up, and they seize all the posts of government. Now, unlike the king, the priest, and the noblemen, the newly rich have received no consecration, not even a conventional one, have no prestige, not even ill-founded, have no authority and no preparation for precedence, so that the nation finds itself adrift. Nobody serves the newly rich out of a sense of duty or obeys them out of respect or trust, or imitates them because they inspire affection or admiration. The newly rich can only reign by corruption.

Commerce destroys the earthly and fleshly ties of man, destroys the natural, organic groups in which he was rooted, his father's farm, the parish, the guild. The whirlwind of business grinds the nations down, reduces them to mobs in which each pushes his way through the others without knowing them, like fish after their prey.

Commerce knows the old adage, "Divide and rule." It sets up the régime of separation, and puts a great gulf between the producer and the consumer, a gulf it alone can bridge, so that it seems to be almost a benefactor, not to say a saviour. This ringmaster does admirable conjuring tricks, snatching the commonest objects from under our noses and putting marvelously packed exotic ones in their place. Thanks to his foresight, on any beach on the coast of England you can open a can of fish that has come, more than fresh, from Japan; in any Devonshire village, not more than ten yards from the cowshed, you can unwrap a pat of butter that has come all the way from New Zealand.

You might think that such complicated carryings on are superfluous, but it only takes a crisis (which, by the way, never fails to occur) to show that they have become indispensable and that our lives depend on them. As soon as man acquires intelligence, bread earned in the sweat of his brow is no longer enough for him. He learns to play, and to feed himself by means of the game.

Commerce does its utmost to decorate, disguise, adulterate, and falsify produce, wherein a common feature of play is apparent: contempt of the real and a taste for subterfuge and travesty.

Under color of giving goods a more attractive appearance and making them easier to conserve, transport, and handle, it plays about with them until they have become something quite different, or takes something quite different and makes it represent or replace the product desired. This is how fancy materials have come into existence: sheet iron, chromium, nickel, concrete, galalith, celluloid, and plastics, the fantasies of stinginess which confer on things of this century their false, empty, mean look, the tinsel glory of the new truths. In this domain, the inventions of the mischievous attain a kind of burlesque poetry; sausages are made from sawdust, cream from horse albumen, coffee from rotten figs, silk from glass, wool from milk, and even butter from water.*

Real wood is made into imitation wood. Poultry is reared on petroleum, calves fattened with injections, hens made to lay square eggs ready for transport.† Similarly, opinion is formed and deformed by publicity and the press, and played about with at their convenience.

The country in which trafficking prospers most is reduced to feeding on canned stuff, a guarantee of weediness for generations to come. Sugar and rice are spoiled by bleaching, drinks (and I don't mean alcohol, but harmless syrups and lemonades) are colored and flavored with violent poisons. But it is all grist to the mill of commerce, and doubly so for the chemical and pharmaceutical trades. Bread has been attacked with singular insistence. The only bread to be found in shops, white bread, is one of the most pernicious of adulterated foods. As for real bread, the bread that gave

* A German substitute, derived from hydrogen, that must be eaten raw because, if you heat it in a pan, it returns to its original state and disappears.
† Soft-shelled eggs laid directly into boxes (in America).

our forefathers their strength and no doubt something of their virtues, the bread Christ broke with his men, saying, "This is my flesh," the bread of truth, which is of the color of the earth, we do not even remember its taste. The very earth itself has been attacked. Drugged with chemical "fertilizer," it has been forced and exhausted until henceforward it can bring forth only insubstantial crops laden with unknown poisons. And while we try out ever more unnatural and untraditional methods of farming, the desert gains yearly on arable land. The water in our rivers has been fouled and turned into poison. But all that is nothing to what is in store, since commerce will shortly have replaced farm produce (so extremely cumbersome and coarse) by nourishing pills (so practical, healthy, and ideal), scientifically seasoned, of course, with vitamins.

Of all meats, the one with the least body in it and therefore the most adventurously advantageous to commerce is surely diversion. For an intelligent man, bread is not enough, as you well know, O Business Men, and if you are realists and want to get fat, feed him on Nothingness, for that is what he likes most of all. Feed something quickly to the gaping idle thrown into the streets in their millions by the whims of fortune and mechanized labor. The public is a big baby: show him your rattles. He wants nothing better than to be attracted, he has nothing better to do than to lose himself, nothing more pressing than to flee himself. To be diverted is to be as if one were not. It is to be relieved of one's being and fritter away into nothingness, as Beelzebub, King of the Flies, who reigns over the vulgar and the mob, well knows. And you, since you have taken a bigger bite of "Knowledge" than the others, play at making them play, and turn the merry rout to your advantage. Assail the passer-by on all sides with garish posters, winking lights and stunning noise, mirrors and shopwindows. As soon as you have caught his eye, allot him a shiny article. He will give not a thought to the price: diversion puts him into the mood for spending. To him, it is just something that has caught his fancy, a trinket, a bauble, to you, hard cash. Inveigle him into a bar where the music—syrupy, saccharined, or drugged—will help him to swallow the alcohol, and the alcohol to swallow the music, and the whole mixture pours coins into your cashbox. Theaters, novels, nightclubs, jukeboxes, dives, music halls, cinemas, magazines, the radio going full blast on all the floors of all the houses, produce and reproduce diversion, and even when you sell it cheap, you are always the winner. This is also the business of the big press, for which whole forests are ground down into paper pulp.

So get ready for the triumphs of World Fairs and erect Eiffel Towers, hollow monuments, in honor of the goddess Diversion that she may always be propitious to you.

Do not despise elegance or think lightly of vanity, which is not at all vain for the industrious entertainer. Bits of finery, make-up, perfumes, curls, real or false jewelry, even buttons are things of importance.

Institute lotteries and auction sales if you want to be sure of more-than-winning every round. Do not forget racing, where fortunes veer and vanish in exemplary style. But above all, give every encouragement to what, from an old French word duly barbarized, is now called *sport*. Give your emphatic approval to every speech to the effect that sport is beneficial to the health of the nation, and indeed even to the health of the young, and at least try to benefit from it yourself. It is the sign of one of the sores of the century.

The sore of which sport is the sign is the degradation of work. It is because there is no longer any joy in work that games are exalted to this point. Sport was invented by a privileged class to ward off the bodily degeneration that lies in wait for the idle. Some of these sports, such as ball games, cycling, and boxing, have become popular crazes because even manual work has been mutilated by the factory just as the intellect has been emptied by office work.

As for the sports practiced by professionals, brutes who are celebrated as heroes and models, they are reduced, for the people, to aggressive, sedentary heat, senseless and unhealthy excitement. However, it is an excellent stimulus to international rivalry and sound preparation for war.

And business men, if you are in earnest, don't forget fun! From political caricature to smutty songs, from the circus to the operetta, from movie cartoons to humorous novels, laughter is a mine that gives rich returns. *Laughter is the ecstasy of diversion.* The public who swallow this bait will never have enough of it, for they are totally empty.

A monkey pulling another monkey's tail puts on a suitably preoccupied look. Do as he does when you are hanging on the telephone and convince us all, yourself included, of the excessively serious nature of your business.

## NOON AT TWO O'CLOCK

The French say of a stupid person who complicates things uselessly that he searches for noon at two o'clock. All players do this, since the rule of the game is to multiply mock obstacles.

Our civilization could be defined as that which found noon at one o'clock. In order to justify such a strange thing and to preserve an appearance of gravity (Woe unto him who laughs in the middle of a game of poker!), we have taken care to put forward an economic explanation. In times of war or crisis, or as an effect of surprise, this maneuver has no doubt made it possible to get all the shops in the land to close one hour earlier and thus save electricity. But as soon as a misuse of language becomes customary, it loses its point. The only reason one can find for it is that people have such a taste for falsification that nothing is safe from them, not even the sun.

## THE MONEY GAME

Since money serves as the measure of the market value of things, and all money bears the mark of the state that guarantees it, what is one to think of a state that makes a forger of itself? To put it at the mildest, the liberal régime, which is that of gamesters, has ended up by raising fraud to the level of a state institution. Nowadays, every government in turn plays around with the bank-note printing machine to falsify its accounts and hand on its fraudulent finance to its successor. But the trick being too well known to deceive anyone, it becomes a gratuitous and conventional pretense, a game that amuses nobody. The game consists in degrading the values which are the basis for measuring values, like a dog chasing its own tail. This juggling affects signs only. What was called one is now called ten, what was called ten is called a hundred, and at the end of the farce everyone is a millionaire and no better off than before. This practical joke leaves a general impression of sliding into a vacuum. Among the multitude of financial experts in search of the stroke of genius that will restore confidence, I wager that not one will hit upon the only means of solving the problem instantaneously—calling a dollar a dollar and bringing as much gold as is necessary out of the vaults of the bank where it lies useless so long as it is buried.

But these are innocent games compared with the devaluation of morals and the degradation of man.

In our world, we are each as dependent on others for the satisfaction of the least of our needs as a child at the breast is on its mother, yet all surrender, all gratitude, all kindness are rigorously excluded from this dependence. Each looks upon others merely as a means of serving his own ends. The keenest and finest joy he can have of his neighbor is to beat him by playing according to the rules. Money then becomes the sole support of his life, the sole link between men, the sole measure of all things and of man himself. Good and evil are reduced to profit and loss, intelligence to cunning, happiness to possession, honor to spending, and time, which is our lives, "is money," as now say those who sell their own and those of other men.

## THE GAME OF PROGRESS

To the fever of Business we owe the canker of Progress. This is a unique case. Indeed, it is the finest, most highly reputed, interesting, widely studied, and envied canker in the world. Thanks to the stranglehold of machinery and chemical disintegration, it opens up to future humanity limitless prospects of Hell on earth and collective suicide.

# THE PLEASURE OF LOVE

Without doubt it is the act of love and procreation that has occasioned the most interesting elaborations, to the extent of doing everything and the opposite of everything.

Male and female created He them, and commanded them to multiply and spread. The work of the flesh is therefore His will. And His kindness wills that it should be accompanied by beauty, joy, and plenitude, as the whole of nature testifies every spring.

Man, however, cannot follow nature in this, not as a result of Original Sin, but even earlier, by virtue of his dignity as a conscious child of God. For the nature of nature is profane, whereas the nature of man is religious.

Marveling at the act of love and procreation is one of the two sources of religion, the other being stupefaction at the discovery of death.

At the instant when the spark of procreation flashes through him, man feels himself transported by a power he experiences but has no knowledge of, a power he recognizes as a mystery.

Therefore, he has no right to the act of love and procreation unless its motive be love, its purpose to beget, its condition religious consecration.

Seeking one's own enjoyment in the carnal act, instead of spending oneself in it for the joy of union and to go beyond one's own life, is indeed biting into the fruit and stealing the gift.

Now, it is because pure pleasure (purely animal pleasure) is neither permitted nor possible to him that man turns toward lechery. For his knowledge—capable of conferring on love the fullness of its meaning, which is marriage and sacrament—gives him, in keeping with the logic of his fall, the means to elude love's solemn bonds and also to elude, as a troublesome accident, the fecundity which is the natural reason for union, and even to elude that union in the heart which is never exempt from grave anxiety and sorrow. Thus it urges him to the pursuit of pleasure, while enabling him also to elude—if his means suffice—fatigue and disgust.

But bodily orgasm, being what it is, intense and disappointing, and lasting as long as it lasts—the space of an instant —can only be augmented by dreaming and stagesetting. Hence the rich furnishings and decoration of drawing room and garden, table and couch; hence jewelry and dress, perfume and song, dancing and feasts and travel. Worldly fatuity, insolent jubilation over fashionable scandal, the thrills of risk and intrigue may be added to these, to make an imaginary stir in emptiness.

This is where the wealth of nations melts, the superfluous wealth that seems to be the supreme flower and highest peak of their achievement. Here civic virtue, family structure, and religious faith melt. While it is true that the imagination of love's pleasure gives rise to some social evils such as prostitution and the abandoning of children to state orphanages, it is also the source of the brilliance of civilizations, for like the waters of a fountain, they fascinate us by their dying fall.

# THE BEAST THAT ROSE UP OUT OF THE SEA

*And I stood upon the sand of the sea, and saw a beast rise up out of the sea, having seven heads and ten horns, and upon his horns ten crowns, and upon his heads the name of blasphemy.*

*And the beast which I saw was like unto a leopard, and his feet were as the feet of a bear and his mouth as the mouth of a lion: and the dragon gave him his power, and his seat, and great authority.*

*And I saw one of his heads, as it were wounded to death; and his deadly wound was healed: and all the world wondered after the beast.*

*And they worshipped the dragon which gave power unto the beast: and they worshipped the beast, saying, Who is like unto the beast? who is able to make war with him?*

*And there was given unto him a mouth speaking great things and blasphemies; and power was given unto him to continue forty and two months.*

*And he opened his mouth in blasphemy against God, to blaspheme his name, and his tabernacle, and them that dwell in heaven.*

*And it was given unto him to make war with the saints, and to overcome them: and power was given him over all kindreds, and tongues, and nations.*

*And all that dwell upon the earth shall worship him, whose names are not written in the book of life of the Lamb slain from the foundation of the world.*

*If any man have an ear, let him hear.*

*He that leadeth into captivity shall go into captivity: he that killeth with the sword must be killed with the sword. Here is the patience and the faith of the saints. (Rev. 13:1–10)*

The sea, that indeterminate watery mass, shimmering, cold, and alien, swollen with storms and gross with riches, is Matter with its engulfing chasms and changing surface of phenomena.

And the Beast that rises up out of the sea is the Science of Matter, a monster with shiny scales and tentacles. It has seven heads, for there are seven gifts of the spirit and seven deadly sins. And there we have seven times as many heads as are needed to understand all there is to know: that we are dealing with a Beast.

And ten horns sprout from the seven heads, how, we cannot tell. But what does it matter if we cannot figure out their uneven distribution, so long as we translate the figures into thoughts?

A horn, in biblical language, means a victorious force. And this confused profusion of victorious forces rises out of the multiple heads that stick out of the Beast that rises up from the sea.

And each of its forces ensures its prestige and royalty (a crown), and it achieves the total royalty of ten crowns.

And its heads bear names of blasphemy, for this octopus that was bred in glacial darkness and thrusts and swells itself up in tumult, this many-headed unwieldy octopus is an insult to God who is One and our Father in Heaven.

Voracious is the Beast Science. Like hunger, its curiosity goes seeking whom to devour, grabs and reduces. Moreover, it panders to man's bestial cravings and capricious vices and enables the beast in him to triumph over all the rest and so become a scourge for the whole earth. Voracious is the Beast Science. "The beast which I saw was like unto a leopard, and his feet were as the feet of a bear and his mouth as the mouth of a lion." It has the crawling suppleness of the leopard, which is spotted like a serpent, the heaviness of the bear, and the pride of the lion.

The Dragon, says the text, gave it its power, and its throne, and great authority.

In the preceding chapter (12:9) we learn the Dragon's name. He is called the Devil or Satan, by whom the whole earth is seduced.

Here, scientists are going to burst out laughing as one man. They are not the kind of people who believe in the Devil. But to affirm that he does not exist is the greatest service one can render him: it is to grant him complete domination over oneself, for never is he freer to do his work than when he wears the mask of nonexistence.

But joking and figures of speech apart, say the scientists, let us speak clearly and in the language of today. It is true that we do not believe in the Devil or in his Celestial Opposite, but we do believe in Truth. It is Truth we desire, love, and pursue with detachment, intrepidity, and perseverance. The good or bad applications men make of it do not concern us: we are not responsible for them. The search for Truth is a severe, almost ascetic, sometimes heroic discipline. And nothing is higher, purer, or more luminous than Truth. It is the major attribute of what is commonly called God.

To which it must be answered that Truth is knowledge of the One, of Self, of Substance, of Life, of the Beginning and the End, in short, of all that science systematically ignores.

# THE NUMBER SIX HUNDRED
# AND SIXTY-SIX

*. . . the name of the beast, or the number of his name . . .*
*Let him that hath understanding count the number of the*
*beast: for it is the number of a man; and his number is Six*
*hundred threescore and six. (Rev. 13:17–18)*

Attempts have been made to interpret this "number of
a man" as a proper name and some have seen it as the name
of Nero, but the explanation is shortwinded. It is the full
meaning of the number Six that must be considered.

One is the Principle.

Two, creation, the creature, Division.

Three, Perfection: Distinction in Unity.

Six is made up of two opposite trinities; the perfection
of Three is in its elements, the weakness of Two in the co-
hesion of the whole.

This number therefore marks the point where high
virtues, noble ambitions, and the finest discoveries of genius
confront each other two by two to bring about a disaster as
great as their grandeur.

This number is truly the sign of our times, when trouble
springs not so much from our weaknesses as from the estim-
able truths in which we believe and our courage in defending and imposing them.

From these fine truths come the technological and social
progress which present themselves under such alluring colors
that it is difficult to detect in them the cause of the greatest
scourges.

Which is the reason for the apostle's warning: "Here is
Wisdom."

Yet it is obvious that the world swings from war to revolution only to swing back to even more total war.

It is also obvious that war becomes more total and bondage more complete as science and machinery progress.

Why, then, is it so difficult to link the two things in a single concept and see that they are one and the same thing and that we must guard against it?

The reason is that "Here is Wisdom," and wisdom is rarer than ever in this century.

And the figure of the number of the Beast, consisting of three Sixes in a row, as if in diminishing perspective, seems to indicate that it designates our epoch as a whole, together with the cascade of catastrophe proper to it on the three planes of the world. And that it is pointless to attach it to a proper name.

But then, what can *it is the number of a man; and his number is Six hundred threescore and six* mean? (We are warned twice of the difficulty of the question.)

We all know that the number of a man, a "living soul," that is to say, an animal, is Six, since he was created on the sixth day.

The number 666 surpasses him, but on the same level, by a dwindling repetition. Six goes on "sixing" in a vain attempt to surpass itself and reach Seven.

To say that the number 666, that of the diabolical Beast, is *the number of a man*, is to say that man has tried to surpass himself outwardly and on the level of nature, and on all levels of nature. Therein lies the cause of the catastrophe.

# OWNERSHIP

Whereas the Knowledge-of-Good, acquired from Original Sin, urges man into a systematic search for pleasure, which, the further he pursues it, leads him into ever greater perplexity, friction, frustration, and danger, so the Knowledge-of-Evil (that is to say, fear of every loss and privation possible) surrounds him with defenses in which he remains imprisoned.

Fear of want is a product of the intellect. It cannot come from the senses since its concern is for a lack, and a lack which is not felt but conceived possible. It comes, therefore, from the evil of "knowing." And it covers everything human with defenses called ownership.

To possess is not a natural gift but a social and rational fact.

The possession of goods concerns not only the owner and the object owned but also all the non-owners who must acknowledge that they are excluded from it. Now, while it is a social fact, its negative and separative character should be noted at the start. For it is indeed ownership that has made the earth bristle with barriers and walls and raised all kinds of visible and invisible obstacles between men.

If it is the work of reason, we can only wonder at the irregularity of its proliferation, and wherever it abounds, it is called Fortune, which means chance, the opposite of reason.

Truly it is the bitten fruit of Knowledge. And already we are becoming accustomed to see the serpent's promises reversed as they are fulfilled.

# WHY A GOOD IS CALLED A GOOD

A good is a possessed object that is a cause of enjoyment.

Past enjoyment is no longer anything. But the object recognized by reason as a good keeps its name forever. The good thenceforth takes on objective consistency which all may observe and all must acknowledge. The quantity of good condensed in the object is even measured with precision.

This measurement is called value. To human reason alone is it given to rise to judgments of value.

Indeed, no animal is capable of showing as much interest in the object of future, or merely probable, or just possible, or even improbable pleasure. No animal shows as much, if not more interest in an object than in what satisfies its present need. No animal is capable of cluttering itself with an object that once served it but no longer serves. No animal is capable of cherishing an object for the sole reason that it is difficult for anyone else to possess. No animal is capable of getting pleasure from an object for the good reason that other people like it but cannot have it.

Indeed, a very high degree of "the Knowledge" is necessary for so much refinement of absurdity.

Yet reason looks upon possession as necessary and upon wealth as good, and morality respects and approves property.

## RICHES AND POVERTY

—Hi, man! What do you have?

—A lot of money.

—What do you do with it when you keep it?

—I count it and count on it. I know I'll get something out of it. So I count it again and look at it.

—Do you look on it as something very useful?

—Yes, very useful!

—When is it of use to you?

—When I spend it.

—And when you spend it, do you have it?


There are wealthy men of weight and wealthy men of no weight.

The one I am talking of was of no weight at all.

Wealth enables those who enjoy it to gratify their whims. His whim was to do nothing.

To acquire his wealth, all he had to do was to be born.

His only business was to spend it.

He managed to avoid fatigue and worry by guarding himself from all work and any undertaking.

He managed to avoid the contagion of sadness by keeping the wretched out of his sight.

He managed to avoid tears and trouble by guarding himself from loving.

He managed to pass from pleasure to pleasure without accident and almost without interruption.

Then, one day, he unexpectedly killed himself.

People were astonished. They searched what hidden event could have caused such despair.

But in vain. His friends knew that he had been dead for a long time, wandering in the shallow hell of endless boredom.

Boredom is the void found by the seeker who wants to lose himself in pleasure.

The heart dissipated by pleasure crumbles into dust.

Every distraction distracts a particle from his being. Boredom is the mean abyss of meaninglessness.


And that poor Poor Man!

Possessed by the wealth he does not possess.

Gnawed, devoured by want that is an imaginary evil.

Ill with someone else's good.

All the too-much others have makes him vomit.

Not that he is hungry: he has no appetite.

He has no taste for what he has.

To steal does not enter his head. He's honest, he is!

Gifts he will not accept, for he is proud!

If by a sudden stroke of luck he were suddenly to become rich, goodness knows what he would do.

He himself would not know what to do or say.

That sort of thing always happens to somebody else!

He stares straight at the pretty woman stepping out of the car. He fixes on her his deep, burning eyes.

At her breast where pearls gleam, he stares straight, his deep eyes burning with hate.


Of all magicians, the rich man is the one who has made the most advantageous pact with the Devil.

He has bought the Devil.

He has put him in his pocket.

And now he holds in his hands the signs, spells, and pentacles that bring good things in abundance and make men smile or die, and women sigh.

He can buy everything: the earth and the fruits thereof, travel and foreign skies, adventure or repose, honors and titles, political importance, music, books, pictures, statues, gardens, feasts, dances and the dancing girl, health with drugs, youth and beauty with apparel and cosmetics, oblivion with drink, love with gifts, good repute with alms, immortality with a tomb, and happiness by selling his soul.

To buy something to buy and sell, they have sold their lifetime and all their thoughts, till in the end there is no one left to take advantage of the bargain.

The happiness of the rich is in Having. Woe, then, to Being!

## WEALTH OR IDLENESS

One of the principles of the Science-of-Good-and-Evil is that property is necessary to safeguard the worker and the continuity of work.

"If your field does not belong to you, someone else may come and reap where you have sown," it says.

But the imbrication of fortunes, which is a general consequence of the same principle, has established that in a continuous, legal, regular, and secular manner, he who reaps is precisely he who has not sown or done any work other than that of being the owner of the field.

And it may be that the man who employs a hundred workers in his vineyard or his workshop alone earns as much by doing nothing as his hundred workers do together, with all their strength and all their toil.

—Yes, but he is the head, and a head is worth hundreds of hands.

—Perhaps. Nevertheless, an owner has no need to be a head. Just as he has bought hands, so he can buy intelligence and afford to have a manager, engineers, inspectors, and foremen, and go off and sleep or revel.

This is the case of the great absentee landlords, the society men who go in for perpetual holidays, as it is of big and small "shareholders," so called because they are dispensed from sharing anything, and even sometimes from any notion of the business from which they receive "dividends."*

Sometimes the owner of a small field is its cultivator. But the owner of a huge domain never is. Whence it may be deduced that the more you own, the less you work.

Which does not prevent the Science-of-Good-and-Evil from teaching that "wealth is justified because it is the fruit of work."

But the peculiarity of the Knowledge-of-Good-and-Evil is to deduce without an error of logic or arithmetic evil from good, and to bring forth falseness from truth without knowing how.

So the formula: Wealth is the fruit of labor, by algebraic conversion, has this corollary: The fruit of wealth is idleness. A result verified by experience.

Wealth is the mother of idleness, who is the mother of all vices, as we well know.

* Etymologically, what is to be shared.

It goes without saying that a person of private means is a man who neither earns his living nor serves.

Wealth is a right without duties.

# VALUE

Value is not a product.

Value is not an object.

Value is not in objects.

It is in the heart of man, in his desires and judgment.

It is in the relationship between man and man.

Commercial value is a measure of the intensity of desire, or rather, of the tension between two or several men whose desire converges on an object to their mutual exclusion.

But nothing is as variable as desire, which may change into indifference or even disgust.

And the most ordinary cause for the extinction of desire is its satisfaction.

If desire is easily satisfied, then the object by which satisfaction is procured becomes worthless, even if it answers the strongest and most elementary need. Such, for instance, is the case of air, water, and light.

The object must therefore be rare and difficult to obtain, but possessable.

Every spiritual good is rare and difficult to obtain. That is why it has a value, or rather, why it *is* a value. But it is impossible to own, in the sense that the more commonly it is enjoyed, the more enjoyable it is, and those who desire it desire others to desire and obtain it. Such is shared good, for example, music and truth.

They are of no commercial value. They are without price.

Without price also are the goods that cannot be shared

or exchanged, such as love, or a husband or a wife, or inner freedom, or the fame an author's work brings him, or the authority that comes from virtue coupled with learning.

Only goods that can be shared or exchanged are of commercial value, that is to say, goods of an inferior, a limited, and material order. Their sole value is that attributed to them.

This attributed value increases as their number decreases and is in direct proportion to the number of those who want them and the resistance of their owners.

Now, whereas *to possess* means to defend, *to gain* means to conquer.

In every convergence of covetousness upon an object, conflict is latent. If conflict broke out every time, there would be no society possible.

When conflict breaks out between members of the same society, there are plunder and crime. If it breaks out between two sovereign societies, there is war.

But the constant, tacit conquest that goes on without bloodshed, if not without struggle, is called Gain.

Instead of striking or provoking the party one wants to dispossess, one summons him to a conference and offers him a treaty.

He is paid, and *pacare*, to pay, means to appease.

Which brings us back to what has already been demonstrated: that Trade is halfway between Play and War.

That if trade is a trade, that trade is of the nature of play and war rather than of work. Of the nature of a game of chance. And profit is not bought at the price of toil, as in work, but at the price of genuine risk.

The risk of losing is compensated by the luck of winning.

Such is the honor of the warrior and the honesty of the trader.

# THE POETICS OF MONEY

Money is a false object, tangible but unreal, a possession from which one can get nothing. So long as you have it in your cashbox or your pocket or your hand, it is as nothing.

If you want to benefit from it, you must spend it, and then you no longer have it.

The gold or silver of which money is made no longer belongs to the material world of useful things. It might have been used to make ceremonial dishes, jewels, divine ornaments, or false teeth, but, minted, it is no longer merchandise, for nobody will spend ten dollars to buy ten dollars.

Besides, gold and silver have never had any other real utility than being beautiful. They lend themselves to decorative and symbolic use only. This is what destined them to become the matter of money, just as sound is the matter of speech.

Gold is the sun, blood, and substance of things, for things are light hardened into a crust.

Silver is the moon, water, sap, and the milk of nature.

This is not a question of appearances and literary comparison, but, if philosophers and alchemists are to be believed, of analogy inherent in the substance of things and proved by the transmutation of black matter into living gold. Chinese doctors restore vigor and peace to a sick body by means of two needles, one of gold, the other of silver. The solar needle stimulates, the silver one calms.

Moreover, gold is rare and concentrates great value in little space. All the toil of mining, riddling of riverbeds, exploration, conquest, discovery, and transmutation, these mainsprings of research and the history of nations, have not succeeded (fortunately) in making it lose its value; and as often as its bulk increases in the world, increasing trade in the same degree, its value remains remarkably steady.

It is unalterable and can be buried in the earth or even in water without being attacked by rust or worms.

Gold is always the same wherever it comes from and the differences between one gold and another are due to alloy and nothing else.

It is divisible, and the price of each part is proportionate to its weight, which is not the case with diamonds and other stones.

All these qualities are conveniences which justify its use, but they are also meanings which contribute to its cosmic significance.

Thus the square-headed business man, the fish-eyed financier, and the trafficker who boast that they believe only in what they can touch unwittingly pay tribute to primitive religions, beliefs, magic, mythical and mystical traditions, and the miser* blindly sacrifices to an unknown god.

Just as the eye is the eye and light of the body by its pupil, so gold and silver become money only if they bear the stamp, the effigy, the name, number, and roundness of the astral disk.

This sovereign signature consecrates the money and elevates it from the world of things to the world of signs.

It is a thing that signifies other things, but, above all, signifies rights and powers in the order of human relations. Metal has become *specie*, a word that means appearance, beauty, and reflection.

That men attach themselves to these conventional sym-

---

* Miserliness, "which is also idolatry," says St. Paul.

bols of possible advantage more strongly than to objects and the pleasures of the senses or the moment, more strongly than to loving, resting, or going for a walk, reveals in the most stupid a high degree of abstract imagination—unwitting, senseless, perverted, and stunted though it be. This is one of the instances in which one can lay one's finger on the nature of the Knowledge-of-Good-and-Evil and its difference from knowledge.

If money is a language, unlike speech, it does not aim at agreement and does not establish communication between men but achieves the separation of payer and payee.

If it is a numerical system, its precision, unlike that of science, is incapable of any truth. Being at the same time a thing and the sign of another thing, its peculiar mode of representation is replacement. It represents the absence of what it represents.

If money is the expression of a right, it is a right of fact and chance, a right without justice.

Money is the official pass to every abuse.

It is a way of grabbing things by means of men and finally of grabbing men by means of things.

It is the language of trickery, as speech is that of intelligence.

If we do not want to falsify—or rather, if we want not to falsify—all our relations with our neighbor, the best use we can make of money is to do without it as much as possible.


## STATES OF ECONOMIC MATTER

When economic matter—money or merchandise—is in its liquid state, it cannot be allowed to congeal or stagnate, for should it cease to flow, or flow more slowly, the resulting damage would be almost as bad as scarcity.

This applies to currency, mass-produced articles, and, above all, perishable foods.

But landed property is wealth in its solid state: land, building sites, buildings, and establishments. The ruin of an estate is called its *liquidation.*

Money in its solid state is known as capital. Whereas currency is never worth more than it costs, money amassed takes on new value by virtue of its mass, which is all the rarer the bigger it is. Although water and ice are of the same substance, they cannot be used for the same purpose. This is also the case with money, which, in its liquid state, can only be spent; but condensed into capital, enables property to be acquired, businesses to be set up and managed, and in consequence entitles one to the fruits. While the sleeping partner receives more than a laborer (although it is harder work to wield a spade than to hand over even a big sum of money), and more than an engineer (although the possession of millions of dollars is not such proof of intelligence as the possession of a diploma), this is not because he has forced everyone to pay him tribute, but because his assistance (no less indispensable than that of the others) was probably more difficult to obtain. If there were not so many workers, and if capital were not so scarce, wages would obviously be higher and unearned income lower.

# THE PRIEST AND THE CASHIER

Two things fill me with admiration: the priest at the altar and the cashier in the bank.

When the priest goes up to the altar, he is more richly

arrayed than any well-dressed fashionable man, better adorned than a king, and there are more eyes turned on him than on any famous actor. Whether he be handsome or ugly, he is always splendid to behold. Whether he be big or small, he is always grand. Yet it never enters the head of any priest to think himself the object of all this homage. He neither struts nor shows off nor waves to the public. The very splendor of his chasuble effaces him.

Gifted man, rightly respected and admired, look and learn! That is how you should behave.


The bank cashier wets his thumb, leafs through the bundles, pins together the notes ten at a time, pushes the bundles over the counter, piles others up and slips them into drawers or trolleys. Whether he has dealt out 20 million in one forenoon or put aside 200 billion, his modest monthly salary remains the same. His heart, his head, his hands retain none of the wealth he handles.

O rich man, observe him! Consider his ways and be wise!


## THE "LABOR-SAVING" MACHINE

If people today are not convinced of the unsatisfactory character of a system which has led them from crisis to crash, from bankruptcy to revolt, and from revolution to conflagration; which spoils peace and makes it busy and full of care; which makes war a universal cataclysm, almost as disastrous for the conqueror as for the conquered; which takes the sense out of life and the value out of effort; which consummates the disfigurement of the world and the debasement of its inhabitants; if people today blame no matter whom for the great evils that are overwhelming them and attribute the cause of them to all and sundry except the development of the machine, then one can only conclude that no one is deafer than the man who will not hear.

Their childish admiration for the shiny toys they play with, their fanatical exaltation of the idol they have forged and to which they are ready to sacrifice their children, have turned their heads and blinded them to the obvious, since they continue to believe that the unlimited progress of the machine will usher in an age of gold.

Leaving aside the upheavals that the progress of the machine is constantly inflicting on human institutions, let us consider only the advantages by which it tempts the fool: it saves time and labor, it produces abundance, it multiplies exchanges between the nations and brings them into closer contact, and it will eventually ensure perpetual leisure for all.

If it is true that it saves time, how is it that in countries where the machine is master, one sees only people who are pressed for time? Whereas in countries where men do everything with their hands, they find time to do everything, as well as time to do nothing, to their hearts' content?

If it is true that it saves labor, how is it that whenever it reigns, people are busy, harnessed to unrewarding, fragmentary, boring tasks, hustled by the rhythm of the machine into doing jobs that wear a human being out, warp him, bewilder and weary him? Is this saving of trouble worth the trouble?

If it is true that it produces abundance, how is it that wherever it reigns, there also reigns in some well-hidden slum the strangest, most atrocious misery? How is it that if it produces abundance it cannot produce contentment? Overproduction and unemployment have been the logical accompaniment of the machine whenever it has been impossible to throw the surplus into some hole or devour it in some war.

If it is true that it has increased exchange and brought people into closer touch, it is little wonder that the people in question feel unprecedented irritation with each other. There is nothing more calculated to make me hate my neighbor and him hate me than forcing me upon him in spite of his will and mine. This may be regrettable, but it is only human. Forced contact does not engender union. It is a great pity, but that is the way of nature.

Finally, even if it were possible to avoid all these disasters, God knows how, and relieve man of all hard work and ensure perpetual leisure for him, then all the damage that the progress of the machine has caused by ruin, revolution, and war would become insignificant compared with the ultimate scourge: humanity deprived of all bodily toil.

The truth is that man needs work even more than he needs a wage. Those who seek the welfare of the workers should be less anxious to obtain good pay, good holidays, and good pensions for them than good work, which is the first of their goods.

For the object of work is not so much to make objects as to make men. A man makes himself by making something. Work creates a direct contact with matter and ensures him precise knowledge of it, as well as direct contact and daily collaboration with other men; it imprints the form of man on matter and offers itself to him as a means of expression; it concentrates his attention and his abilities on one point or at least on a continuous line; it bridles the passions by strengthening the will. Work, bodily work, is for nine-tenths of humanity their only chance to show their worth in this world.

But in order that work itself, and not just payment for it, shall profit a man, it must be human work, work in which the whole man is engaged: his body, his heart, his brain, his taste. The craftsman who fashions an object, polishes it, decorates it, sells it, and fits it to the requirements of the person he intends it for is carrying out human work. The countryman who gives life to his fields and makes his flocks prosper by work attuned to the seasons is successfully accomplishing the task of a free man.

But the worker enslaved in serial production, who from one second to another repeats the same movement at the speed dictated by the machine, fritters himself away in work which has no purpose for him, no end, no taste, no sense. The time he spends there is time lost, time sold. He is selling what a free man does not sell: his life. He is a slave.

The problem is not how to sweeten the lot of the proletarian so as to make it acceptable to him, but how to get rid of the proletariat, just as we got rid of slavery, since the proletariat is indeed slavery.

As for the whole nations who are doomed to idleness, what is to be done with them, what will they do with themselves?

People will reply that the state (and if you don't know what the state is, I shall tell you: it is mechanized Providence), which will have solved the problem of work by complete industrialization, will then only have to solve the problems of leisure and education. It will plan games and entertainment and will distribute learning to all.

But the pleasures of men without work have always been drunkenness and mischief. The state can offer them educational pleasures for all it is worth, they will still prefer drunkenness and mischief. The games will then have to become compulsory and for many will cease to be games and turn into discipline and duties, falsifications of work from which no good can come. It would have been better to plan work.

But there is a pleasure dearer to man than work, dearer than drunkenness and mischief, that of shouting "Down with——!" and setting fire to everything. That is a game which will quickly replace all others in the mechanized Paradise.

If the misfortunes that overwhelm even civilized people today finally prove to them, by *reductio ad absurdum*, that they must turn their hopes elsewhere, they will have been of some use after all.

In Europe, in America, and even in Japan, techniques are continuing their progress, but the Religion of Progress, thank God, is beginning to recede.

One no longer hears the paeans and chants of glory that accompanied the rising of coal smoke and balloons in the nineteenth century.

There is no sign of any serious attempt at deliverance in any of these countries, but there are at least some glimpses of clearsightedness, and grave doubts about tomorrow.

Men are carried along now, not by the initial impulse of their faith in progress, but by its continuing course and their submission to fatality. "Whatever you may say," they tell you, "you can't go against the laws of history and economy. There is no turning back now."

And here you see how strong-minded people who have rebelled against all belief, and claim to be guided in all they do solely by their courage and intelligence, lose their critical faculties and let themselves be led by the nose when superstition is artificial and learned and bears the name of History or Economy, and resign themselves to a fatality which is nothing other than their own stupidity and obstinacy.

Drought, floods, earthquakes, pain, old age, and death are fatalities against which it is senseless to protest. History and economy, being man-made, are done and undone with equal ease. The only thing that makes them ineluctable is to believe them to be so. It is senseless to resign oneself to them instead of working to change them.

If machines could be used reasonably, within limits, and their progress controlled, there would indeed be no drawback to putting them to work. One can very well use machines, provided one can do without them.

If a machine is useful, then use it; if it becomes necessary, then it is your urgent duty to throw it away, for it will inevitably catch you up in its wheels and enslave you.

The machine enslaves, the hand sets free.

## THE COMMUNITY OF THE ARK

The Ark might be reproached with being engaged in spiritual preparation and teaching more than in specific public action.

Our intervention in public affairs has never been more than testimony—symbolic rather than successful.

To *do*, one must first *be*, and that is what we are attempting. Spiritual preparation is not a means for us, but an end in itself more important than any outward manifestation or victory. Bringing man face to face with God and with him-self is in itself desirable. If the Tree of Life is found again, acts will fall from it like ripe, good fruit.

The most efficient action, the most significant testimony to nonviolence and truth is not so much handing out tracts in the street and talking to crowds, or going from door to door, leading walks and campaigns, invading bomb factories, fasting in public, braving the police, undergoing assault and imprisonment( all of which we find right to do on occasion and do willingly), as living. Living a life that is whole, and in which everything has the same sense, from prayer and meditation to plowing for our daily bread, from teaching the doctrine to treating dung, from cooking and singing to dancing round the fire.

Showing that a life free from violence and wrongdoing is possible (violence may be hidden as well as brutal; may be legal and authorized as well as illegal). Showing that such a life is not more difficult than a life of gain, nor more un-pleasant than a life of pleasure, nor less natural than "ordi-nary life."

Finding the nonviolent response to the problems that have always beset man, such as:

—Can there be an economy that lends itself neither to pres-sure nor abuse?

—Can children be educated in nonviolence? Can nonvio-lence be taught to people of all ages?

—Can authority be nonviolent, neither dependent on force nor carrying privilege?

—Can justice be nonviolent?

—Can there be justice without punishment, or punishment without violence?

—Can agriculture and animal breeding be nonviolent?

—Can there be nonviolent medicine? Nonviolent psychiatry? A nonviolent diet?

And to begin with, have we rid our religious life of all violence, even in word and thought, even hidden or disguised?

## The Elements of a Nonviolent Economy

In the light of our views on the Spirit of Lucre and the Spirit of Play, it will come as no surprise.

That we endeavor to draw our living directly from the earth by the work of our hands, avoiding, as far as we can, the use of machines and money;

That we endeavor not to violate and break the link God and nature have put between what the mouth asks for and what the two hands can produce;

That we reduce our desires to our needs, and our needs to the extreme so as to free ourselves from excessive toil;

That we sell the surplus of what we produce for ourselves, but never buy in order to sell or profit from mere exchange;

That we pool what resources we have that can serve the community, and give up the rest; but our communities remain poor and do not accumulate more than is needed for the year's supplies;

That as far as we can, we observe the golden rule never to pay anybody and never to let anyone pay us;

That we exploit no man, even if he asks us to, and refuse to become the accomplices of any profiteer, even if it might be convenient. For in the same measure as we are dedicated to service, we refuse servitude;

That we try to exploit nothing at all, neither animals nor plants nor the earth. We live, and let live, and help to live;

That in the practice of any craft, we are less concerned

with the quantity of the product than with its quality, and less concerned with the product than with the craftsman;

That we do not consider work and craftsmanship as something external to personal and spiritual life, but consider the work of the hands as a sacred act. It is also an act of life. So we want it to be interesting, varied, harmonious, strengthening, instructive, and edifying;

That the lowest and most menial tasks are shared by all, and foremost by our leaders, so that nobody is demeaned or burdened by them;

That every craftsman among us knows and carries out his craft from beginning to end and makes the whole object, from the raw material to the final decoration. Nobody is harnessed to a fragmentary task or makes less than the whole object for fear of his becoming less than a man. For it is by making things that a man makes himself. Nobody among us will be limited to a single craft, but will possess several, and alternate them. Everybody has to set to and help with farming and gardening according to the season. This is the best kind of work for health and holiness. Let every craftsman seek for the rhythm and the sense of his craft and he will discover secrets lost since the ruin of the guilds.

The Ark is neither a religious order nor a chivalrous order. Nevertheless, it has similarities with both: it is a working order. It is not a brotherhood of monks, but a new people, made up of laymen who have children and bring them up. A people apart, but indifferent to barriers of nationality, class, race, or creed. A people that does not without good reason oppose established national law and authority but considers itself, small though it be in numbers and strength, as free and sovereign, like the nomads of the desert, and vagrant gypsies.

## Elements of Religious Reconciliation

The order is not a religious order. It is not an attempt to set up a new religion. It endeavors to reconcile men, purify their means of existence, orient them toward spiritual life, and initiate them into the ways of wisdom.

The order has no intention of attacking, criticizing, reforming, or replacing any established Church. It lays no claim to bringing revelation of man's last end, and teaches no new form of worship. It cannot therefore clash with the Church, for the good reason that it does not put itself on the same level but below, and does not intend to trespass in the domain of dogma, liturgy, or the sacraments.

The order is like a father whose first care is to honor God. But when one wants to live a holy life, one must first try to be honest and not be pious at someone else's expense.

Men of different religions can agree on these principles and live side by side in deep spiritual friendship, provided they consider that God is One, Unique, and the Same, That-Which-Is, in all that is, and provided they respect the heritage common to all the traditions and abstain from discussion and judgment of the differences between these.

Our rule invites every man to become converted to his own religion, to convert himself, that is to say, to pass from the profane to the religious or inner state. All religions are tolerated in the order, but not intolerance or irreligion.

With nonbelievers we do not argue either, nor do we preach to them. If they come to us, we turn them to contemplation of their own soul. The image of God is there, the Kingdom of Heaven is in the heart. May they see and touch what is. Why should we preach or argue?

## Elements of Political Reconciliation

Seeing that the social problem is fundamentally and definitively solved by patriarchal order, which has remained steadfast since the times of Seth, Enoch, and Melchisedec, we have no part to play in the excitement that sweeps the mob toward bloody revolution. For the same reason, we partake in none of the works, none of the abuses, none of the excitation that lead to war.

We are strictly forbidden to profess political opinions, occupy official posts, or seize power. Not that we turn away from the world's affairs or despise our fellow men or remain indifferent to their want, their servitude and dissension. Our retreat is only a means of seeing events from the distance indispensable to correct judgment and to finding the right way out for all.

The aim of the order is to create, within the nations, little islands of perfect life, not that we think ourselves perfect or set ourselves up as an example, but if, imperfect as we are, and in many ways "the last," we find the garden and Kingdom of Heaven here and now, the demonstration is all the more convincing. Our aim is to multiply these little islands by emigrating from the mother community and turning as many people as possible away from the mad philosophies of our times, and instead of exciting them one against another, class against class, party against party, religion against religion without knowing what may result from the shock, to unite and pacify them here and now, and oppose their peace to the agitation of the world.

This is how the Companions recall their vows every evening after common prayer round the fire lit under the stars:

## The Vows

(The Companions alone say this prayer, arms crossed, hands flat on their breasts.)

God the Eternal, strong, just, and good, let us never forget that we have taken the vow to keep to and advance along the road of the seven accomplishments, which are:

(1) To give ourselves up to the service of our brothers, which begins with the work of our hands, so as at least to burden no one, and find a way out, for ourselves and other people, from the afflictions, the abuses, the servitude, and trouble of this age.

To work on ourselves, to exercise ourselves daily for the possession, the knowledge, and the gift of ourselves.

To work for the growth and upkeep of the order by defending justice with the weapons of justice, to rise to the call at all times, by teaching, missions, and foundations, by hospitality and good neighborship, by care for dignity and beauty, by contribution to the chapter, gatherings, and feast-day celebrations.

(2) To conform to the rules and discipline of the Ark and obey the leaders who serve by their advice and command, and to recall each other to obedience.

(3) To accept full responsibility for our acts; to put right our misdeeds or make up for them; to punish ourselves in place of our Companion should he refuse to admit a wrong and correct it.

(4) To purify ourselves from attachment, from mental dissipation, from pretension, prejudice, rancor, and anger, from indifference, covetousness, and pretense, from our aversion, hate, and connivance, from laziness and cowardice, by fasting and penance, the awakening of conscience and prayer.

(5) To live in a clean, simple, and sober manner, to cherish poverty in order to advance toward detachment and perfect charity.

(6) To speak the truth with courage unless prudence, charity, or respect compel us to silence; to shun fraud, intrigue, and gossip.

(7) Not to afflict any human being nor, if possible, any living creature for pleasure, profit, or convenience. To settle conflict, to check outbursts, and to right wrongs by nonviolence, which is the power of truth; to convince, not vanquish; to reconcile, not dominate; to conquer peace.

Grant us, Lord, to bear our Cross to the end, to know Thee, to love Thee, to serve Thee; in short, to be. Amen.

## A NOTE ON THE TYPE

The text of this book was set in Electra, a type face designed by William Addison Dwiggins for the Mergenthaler Linotype Company and first made available in 1935. Electra cannot be classified as either "modern" or "old-style." It is not based on any historical model, and hence does not echo any particular period or style of type design. It avoids the extreme contrast between thick and thin elements that marks most modern faces, and is without eccentricities that catch the eye and interfere with reading. In general, Electra is a simple, readable type face that attempts to give a feeling of fluidity, power, and speed.

W. A. Dwiggins (1880–1956) began an association with the Mergenthaler Linotype Company in 1929 and over the next twenty-seven years designed a number of book types which include the Metro series, Electra, Caledonia, Eldorado, and Falcon.

Composed, printed, and bound by
The Haddon Craftsmen, Inc.,
Scranton, Pennsylvania.

Typography and binding design by Virginia Tan.